How to Chat up Men

AMY MANDEVILLE

Foreword by

Michael Bywater

SUMMERSDALE

Summersdale Publishers
46 West Street
Chichester
West Sussex
PO19 1RP
United Kingdom

A CIP catalogue record for this book is available from the British Library.

Printed and bound in Great Britain
by Selwood Printing Ltd., Burgess Hill.

ISBN 1 873475 48 9

Original illustrations by Amanda Byfield.

To all the men I have longed for, lusted after, left and lost. If anybody finds one of them please let me know.

Acknowledgments

To all of my lovelies who helped me, whether they know it or not:

The students of Calavaras Union High School, via the (O') Brophy clan; Patrick from The Kennel Copy Center and his Internet pirates; John and Kay Rothwell; Suzi Miles; Kyle Fedderly; Casey Masingale and that other Kyle; Johnny Oliviera with his orgasmic hands and yellow CRX; Peter and Thunder Lockheart; the ill fated Mike Kelly; Angie Gaskins and her silly pygmy of a man; John What's-it; Mr. Kelly- I may just start calling you 'Jim'; Ben Someone-or-other; Ben Chavis PhD; Reed VanRozeboom, because he's family; Alan Brown and short but sexy Shane; Alan and 'I like to watch' Marshall; Alan Hawkins; Christos and his Fridays; Darryls #1 and #2; John Tzinos; Penny, Diane, Peta, Bobbi, Linda, Sue, Karen, Gillian and all of the other hens; Matt Reid, because I will always hate you with all of my heart; Nevin Jay Taylor; Steve Weisman, a short Jew with a funny fetish; Julia and Amanant of the shoddy moral fibre; Chris Graves; Raul '50' Iskandar; Doug and Mike Mclaughlan; Grandma and 'knee sock' Nana; My darling Ryan; Dr.Bob and Nyla Libke; Gordon Powell; John Phillips, Sally and the lot; Karl Prior and Jeremy; Bill and Hill; Lisa Sutherland; Medhat Rafla; Paul Ante and his lovely Laura; Andy and Dennis; Satu 'Lisa' O'Finland; Sophie Hutchins; Manos; Themos; Spiros and Corinna; Demi and Constantinos; Valerie Botting; Helen and Gurmy;

Gary and Alison; Nicole Champoux; Sam Young and his incessant lack of faith; Christi Barnes and Mike Kalmbach; and Shifty, always a comfort and an inspiration.

A big *Gracias* to those of you who had relationships interesting enough to be inspirational.

Efharisto Poli to my family, even if they didn't always get the jokes.

My eternal gratitude to my mother; me but older and with thinner hair.

Donka to the Anthropology Department at CSUF. Where would the world of anthropological trivia be without you?

And some big wet ones for Alastair Williams and Stewart Ferris, my very own pet pig; without whom none of this would ever have brightened a book shelf.

A thousand thank yous, Michael Bywater.

Contents

Scenarios

Foreword

You're probably wondering, 'Does this book work? Does this woman know what she's talking about?'

Yes.

You're looking at the proof of it. What I mean is, I don't do forewords. Ever. I particularly don't do forewords when I'm meant to be finishing a book of my own, having told my publisher that I'd already finished so that I'd have no option but to stock up on typewriter ribbons, tie a damp marsupial around my head and get to work.

Then Amy Mandeville chatted me up.

She did it, initially by letter: a tricky one to pull off, but she managed it. She said all the right things. She told me I was wonderful. She said she adored my mind. She hinted that if I didn't have lunch with her she would go to the silent tomb nurturing a secret sorrow. There was some stuff about Danny Baker, too, which I let pass, and she failed to mention that she hungered for my body, but that was probably just an oversight.

So we had lunch, and she was good at that, too. The confidences. The glances. The body language. The sensual running of a moistened fingertip round the rim of the glass . . . not that she actually <u>did</u> that, but I could tell she wanted to, just as I could tell she yearned (in the innermost core of her being; where else?) for my rippling prose, my muscular adjectives, the pulsing rhythms of my rock-hard, throbbing sentences.

And, as you can see, it worked. I just rolled over and came across.

But (you are wondering) <u>do men actually enjoy being chatted up?</u> The answer is: yes. There are some who don't, but they aren't men. In any case, if everyone follows Miss Mandeville's advice, the poor lambkins will just have to get used to it. It is an idea whose time has come. For far too long, it has been men alone who have endured the terrifying, interminable walk across the floor: the shaking knees, the rapidly-imploding body image, the tongue cloven to the roof of the mouth, the carefully-prepared witty lines crumbling to ashes, the inability even to say 'Hi! By name's Nichael, can get you a drink I?'

It's your turn. And It's no good arguing that our sexual role-playing is rooted in the immemorial mists of evolution. You might say that it's a fine reproduction strategy for men to cluster around with their tongues hanging out, and for women to make their choice. But we have transcended that sort of Neanderthal behaviour - or, if we haven't, at least we've made large parts of it illegal.

So: it's time for women to do their bit. And if, even after reading this book, you still feel unsure that you've really got the hang of it, I will be only too happy to give you my opinion. Why not give me a call? I'll be waiting by the phone.

Michael Bywater

Introduction

Sometime back before even our parents were born, a
certain social system was created, defining the roles
that men and women were to have in the world.
Because of some basic physical differences, women
have spent most of history at the bottom.

You see, men are on average 10% larger than women.
In nature, this makes sense. Women's purpose, as far
as the continuation of the human race is concerned,
is that of a walking uterus. Men are the ones who are
genetically predisposed to do all of those macho things,
like hunting for antelope or, as they think, changing
a cylinder head; their contribution to the perpetuation
of humankind.

Because of the necessity of meat at the table for the
young ones that the females had produced, and the
benefit of physical protection, primitive lads were
getting a whole lot of respect, and got to call most of
the shots. Women were not in a position to argue;
these were not guys you would want to meet in a
dark alley. Besides, have you ever tried hunting woolly
rhino with a toddler in tow?

You don't need me to tell you that a few things have
changed in the last 15,000 years. Before the Industrial
Revolution, women probably had their best chance
of equality with the hunters and gatherers, being
responsible for the gathering of about 90% of the food

stores. Some of the shining stars of the Neolithic era then figured out the advantages of farming, a brawny kind of job, plunging females under men (ironically, it was probably women who put two and two together, as they were the ones digging in the mud every day).

And then it happened: The Industrial Revolution. Suddenly body size had little to do with feeding anybody. In fact, food ceased to be an issue, at least for the majority of the western world. Now it was brain power that mattered, and women have proportionately larger brains than men.

O.K., yeah right, but a survey that came out in a fashion rag 'round about summer of '92 says that 40% of men feel that women are basically less intelligent. Sigh. So, that's why women chatting-up men is kind of a new thing. The men were always expected to take charge. Now we have given ourselves permission potentially to humiliate ourselves completely in an effort to get the three legged beasties to talk to us. It's understandable that we're a little nervous.

What does all of this have to do with chatting-up men? A lot, actually. Chatting someone up successfully has everything to do with how you see yourself, thereby how other people see you. If you are still looking at yourself as a neolithic underdog, so is the local antelope hunter you're making eyes at.

I am not trying to imply, God forbid, that there are not some real differences between men and women. There most certainly are, but it is not a question of being inferior or superior. We each have our own separate sophistications which we should work on exploiting to their fullest. This book is all about slipping women some of those hints. It's time to start taking charge of whom we meet and don't meet. Stop moaning about all of the greasy gits who have been chatting you up lately and how you never seem to meet anybody worthwhile. Start talking to the ones you want to talk to.

Being Single

When I was at university, I worked in the university bookshop between classes to add a little jingle to my pocket. Out of sheer burn-out and general hung-over brain frizzle, I was drawn to the 'under twelve' section, tucked in the corner behind the shoestring-travel-McDonald's-drunken-Europe guides. In my mid-exam stupor, one book in particular grabbed my attention, compelling me to give the shop back three hours worth of wages so that I could own it. The book was *The Missing Piece Meets the Big 'O'* by Shel Silversteen.

It was the story of a little pie-shaped piece looking for a place in which it would fit. Every now and then something resembling Pac-Man would roll by, and the Missing Piece would try to fit into the pie shaped gap. Sometimes it was too big. Other times too small. Sometimes the Pac-Man would put it on a pedestal. And leave it there.

One day the Big 'O' rolled by, pausing to chat with the Missing Piece. The Missing Piece asked the Big 'O' if it was his missing piece. The Big 'O' replied that it was not missing anything, and rolled on alone. This inspired the Missing Piece, who began to flip itself end over end, until eventually its sides wore down and it too became an 'O', rolling on to join the Big 'O' in its travels.

Yes, there is a point.

The point is, to roll along happily with somebody, be sure that you can bounce by yourself first. Don't depend on somebody else to make you whole. All successful relationships between intelligent people are the partnership between two healthy, autonomous personalities. Don't look for your other half, look for a compatible whole.

Don't go through life looking for your *one and only*, the single person on this planet who can make your toes curl in a rip roaring orgasm, and can fill in all your missing squares in the crossword puzzle. In all likelihood there is more than one person in the universe with whom you could happily drift through life. Finding your soul mate is a dangerous expectation which could lead you down the slippery slope of serial monogamy as soon as a guy starts picking at his belly button lint. But then, some people do really well with serial monogamy and it should only be considered a true problem if you intend to have children, as they are far more likely to become neurotic brats who religiously forget Mother's Day as a result of such an unstable situation.

There is little point in denying that the world is a more user-friendly place for single men than single women. Beyond the fact that there is no stigma attached to men chatting-up women, there are no obvious social consequences that go along with anything they do once a woman has been suitably impressed with his wit, charm and, if she's having a particularly bad night, his bold style of belching.

Bachelors have always been entities unto themselves. Audacious, brave, manly - lucky buggers who answer to no one. Sad, but true. Historically, women experienced a different story. There are people alive today who remember a time when to be unmarried, an *old maid*, was shameful indeed. This is not the case now, but there is still a belief that if a woman is single, particularly after a certain age, say sixteen, it's just because she hasn't found the right man.

You must remember all of the valuable parts of being single. You are learning to appreciate you and exactly what makes you tick. You will have more to offer because you have had more opportunity to spend selfish time with yourself and are a more complete, well-rounded person because of it. I can almost guarantee that you will find the capability of creating a better partnership if you can manage to be a good single person.

Let us, for a moment, consider the pros of being single:

• Less laundry

• No in-laws

• Less flatulence

• More crunchy vegetables

• You can leave all of your money to your cat

- Sleeping diagonally on the bed

- No reluctant shoppers

- No stockings (unless you like them)

- No menstruation cracks when you're in a bad mood anyway

- The toilet seat is always down

- You don't have to shave your legs (unless you want to)

- No wet spot to argue about

- You can always stop and ask for directions

Even with these profoundly wonderful advantages to being single, we all know why we will probably want somebody at one time or another, beyond the fact that guys make great midnight foot warmers. It's nice to be a pair. It's pleasant to be someone's favourite, and to have located your own preferred human. At a party you will invariably be within spitting distance of someone who gets your jokes.

In recent years particularly, this whole *being someone's favourite* thing has become a bit tricky. You see, people are programmed to view every new member of the opposite sex they run into as a potential mate. This has always been true, except that now, with the population explosion and the media replete with all its beautiful people, our contact with other humans has broadened enormously. While you might not think this would be a problem, consider studies that show that men (and women) on a subconscious level view all of these electronically reproduced sweethearts as potential mates. Yes, that includes Pamela Anderson. While this might not affect your chances of chatting-up a man (unless Pammy is wiggling around on his lap, in which case you're stupid to try) it does change the formula slightly.

While you're considering your status of bachelorette number 3,001, remember that people are staying single much longer than ever before and are getting divorced at an alarming rate. You can expect your single status to last for a much longer time than either your Mum's or Nan's did. To add to all of this, only 48% of the population is male.

So, girls, since you can't change the numbers, you might as well have fun with them. Don't view every new male acquaintance as the potential father of your children or even as a steady date. Ending a relationship is not a failure, merely a learning experience. You can't expect to get it right the first time or even the first ten times. Yes, every relationship is different, as are all people, but you need to find what's right for you. Give it time.

Revel in your independence and thumb your nose at the rules. After all, you didn't write them.

If you want to play the numbers, the average age for a woman to marry is twenty five, for a man twenty seven. A third of marriages ends in divorce. If you're still keen, read on.

Understanding Men

Back when the universe was drawing up the blueprints for people, it had a brain-storm so amazing it dropped its wax pencil under the table and had to quest for it. In the time the universe spent on its knees cussing and digging, time was flying and the essential deadline was approaching. When the offending pencil was found, the brilliant plan had to be included without the consideration that it really deserved. Because of this the relations between men and women are imperfectly compatible, not only with each other but with the morals and social structures set up by almost every society on the face of the earth. I can't be sure of exactly what the initial inspiration was, but the reality of this poor planning is bound to slap you in the face at least once if you're lucky, a googleplex of times if you're human.

So, here's the plan, shorthand. To ensure diversity within a community, broadening the gene pool, allowing less room for widespread genetic defects, men are programmed to have rabbit-like tastes. Any hole will do, providing that it doesn't have a snake in it. Women are slightly, and I do mean slightly, more discriminating, though we can convince ourselves of almost anybody's worthiness, particularly if we're on the rebound.

Be that as it may, our brains are wired to our genitals differently, and for good, sound reasons. Should our frantic, typically nocturnal thrashings result in offspring, we need to take care of the demanding bit of flesh the midwife hands us. Now, back to our antelope origins (assuming that you weren't naughty, skipping the introduction) it would have been, and quite frankly still is, profoundly difficult to care for a child or children and ourselves by ourselves. We are therefore programmed to stick with a guy, should we have sex with him. Good planning, huh?

Yes, of course this bit of creative wiring can be overcome. The same school of thought that came up with the above conclusions also tells us that we are to stay with our mate for four years if the relationship produces a child at the beginning, or seven years if two children are created in the early days. Remember Marilyn Monroe in *The Seven Year Itch*? I am sure that we can all think of at least a dozen examples for which this scenario is not applicable, but it is real and it's not wholly the guys' fault that they so frequently do unenlightened things with the dangly bit between their legs.

However convenient it would be, this does not entirely excuse their behaviour. Many men, particularly those who are under thirty, seem to be living in suspended childhood. This could be due to the reduced prospects perceived by young people these days and the subsequent likelihood of a longer dependency on the dole, or due to parental mismanagement and therefore a prolonged state of irresponsibility. Many men feel that if they cannot provide for a woman on the financial level, or at least buy his own ice cream, he would rather not be involved at all. Probably for the best; I don't know about you, but I sure as saccharin flavoured coke don't want to get wrapped up in a misguided male ego.

There are many men out there who feel that this childishness, this boyish charm, is somehow acceptable and desirable. Please, don't encourage this, it's a bore. It is also in complete and total contradiction to everything you could ever possibly need or want from a steady partner.

By and large, they're really insecure about the penis. Even more than that they are scared of what we say about them. I like to remind all of my male friends periodically that we do talk about penis size. And then I give them a list of impossible dimensions that a proper pecker is supposed to reach and have them write it on the wall in the bathroom. I hope in this way to promote male hysteria and female worldwide domination. It's a start.

You may recall Freud's now defunct theories about penis envy. What a sick puppy. I find the whole concept of actually wanting an unpredictable sausage between my legs to be very funny. Like I would find it to be a really attractive idea to have something that vulnerable hanging somewhere so conspicuous. Those incredibly sensitive noodles dangling there, easily damaged and mutilated, in need of constant support. A five inch mental and physical barometer. But, silly things, they are so proud, it hasn't even occurred to them how silly they are and how silly they get about them.

They act as though it's so rare, like half of the other people in town don't have one. They sit there with their legs spread apart and this big *I know what you're thinking* leer on their faces, when all that's on your mind is when that stockholder's meeting is tomorrow and if you should *power walk* in the afternoon or play handball with Matts the bimboy in the morning. When was the last time you flashed your fresh box of

Tampax around? It doesn't happen. And you will rarely ever hear a woman say anything like *Oh God, I'm so wet I could bottle my own water,* though men frequently get away with similar cheeky comments regarding their appendage.

Most men aren't nearly as strong as they would like us to think they are. Time and time again it has been shown that it is actually the women who are the stronger of the two sexes. In fact, in terrorist situations, the lawmen are ordered to kill the women terrorists first. Apparently women have more to fight for and more to die for and keep the more lethal mind intact during times of trouble. Think about it, it makes sense for women to be stronger and keep cooler heads. We have always been responsible for the survival of the children. Never think that you are as strong as any man. Know that you are stronger.

Don't laugh, that wasn't funny.

The Basics Of Chatting Up

Back in the good old days when men where men, women were women and snakes were guarding their holes very carefully, chat-up was a piece of cake. A local landowner would come by to negotiate with your dad about a cow, and Pops would toss you in to sweeten the deal. Well, maybe it wasn't quite that bad, but that was the general idea.

In all fairness, up to the time in which 'Wanna cow?' and 'Wanna wife?' were interchangeable phrases, romance and marriage were considered mutually exclusive institutions. In Elizabethan times it was considered the height of poor taste to love your spouse. Love was something you put into poems written under a pen name and sent to your neighbour's wife. That is, if you and your neighbour were of the special sort that could get in to talk to Queen Bess. Think of the word *courting*, which has its origins in this tradition. If your neighbourhood was of the *hunting for the perfect turnip* ilk, romance simply didn't come into it.

The whole practice of pairing-off came about for three rather pragmatic reasons. The first, as touched on earlier, was for the protection of women and children and therefore the perpetuation of we two-legged primates. The second, and even less sugary reason, was the exchange of property (moo) and, for special people, the joining of dynasties.

Now our only good excuses are nookie (a fine reason by itself and if you don't think so, start putting yourself to bed with a decent sex guide) and love. Oh yeah, if you're a bit odd, you might get married because either you want your children to be legitimate, you need a good tax break this year, or you want to move up in the world and the bloke bears a striking resemblance to a ladder. But mostly and thankfully people pair off for the first two reasons which don't necessarily involve marriage. In fact, many women are bowing out of the marriage game altogether in preference for various other levels of coupledom and singledom.

So, chatting-up. As I wrote earlier, it was easier in those naive rustic days, so it would follow that it should be harder now. Mostly we have a rough time because we actually have to do it now, we just had to brush up on our cow milking techniques then.

The first and most important thing about chatting a man up is to make sure that you are completely and totally clear on your ultimate goal. If you are just looking for a night's exercise, fax my friend Shifty on (01243) 786300, any time, day or night. Be sure firstly to think hard about what kind of a person you are and how your mainframe is checking out before you take the plunge. Some people can handle it, others can't. If you're not sure which you are, you'll figure it out very quickly.

If sex is honestly all you want, do yourself a favour and don't exchange phone numbers or stay the whole night. These things smell of some sort of emotional addition to the equation, and neither of you is keen on that odour. Also be clear on exactly why you want this *quickie*. If you're gagging for it, excellent. If you're looking to put an extra notch in your bedpost and are practising safe sex, more power to you. If you are feeling ugly, unattractive, unhappy, unloved or any other words beginning with a *u*, wrap yourself in some cotton wool and watch *Roseanne* repeats. Do not seek a casual sexual encounter whilst in this negative state of mind. You may stop talking to yourself for having passed you such bad advice. Oh, also make sure that this is what the guy is after. A formality at best.

If you are looking for a longer lasting sort of relationship, select your target more carefully, preferably somebody with whom you have already made some sort of verbal contact so you'll know if they're worth it before you go through all of the trouble of opening your mouth. This sort of chatting-up leaves you far more vulnerable, and is apt to be much scarier. Sexy chat-up (chatting-up for aerobic purposes) is very superficial. You're not admitting to anything beyond 'you look like you have a penis and there are no snakes on my person'. Date-type chat-up offers and asks for far more. It's more personal, even if it doesn't sound like it.

When approaching a man, be confident. Don't sidle up to him with your shoulders hunched and your eyes downcast. Be assertive, be flirtatious. Make him believe that you are doing him an incredible favour by speaking to him, while making him feel like he too is wonderful. Don't put so much thought into

what you say as to how you present yourself as a
whole. Worrying about the line is silly. That is the
least of it. If you worry too much about your words
you'll fluff it anyway. Don't be afraid of rejection.
Or success.

Psychology

Don't expect it always to be easy for women to do the chatting-up. This is one of the few arenas in life, besides those obvious ones such as childbirth and breast-feeding, in which women have a real social advantage. Men love to be chatted-up, particularly if they are by themselves. It's a bit trickier if they are with their mates, however, as they will feel honour bound to act all cool and casual and make highly sexist and derogatory comments as soon as you excuse yourself to the loo. Generally though, they are flattered.

Typically, if a man rejects a woman's advances, it's for one of the following reasons. If you have the healthy, well rounded ego recommended in the previous chapter *Being Single* you'll assume that his reason is one of the less painful.

• He's gay

• He's such a catch that he already has a girl and wouldn't cheat on her even for your sexy self

• He has a disease and is too shy to say so

• His girlfriend recently died and she looked just like you

• His girlfriend just dumped him and you don't look a thing like her

- You're not his type

- His mate fancies you

- His mate hates you

- He's impotent

- He doesn't fancy you

- You seem the type to have a snake in you

But you probably won't need this list.

Men are simple creatures; easily flattered. Act (and unless you're at the Cannes Film Festival, you probably will be acting) as if he is the sexiest thing you have ever had the privilege to lay eyes on. Massage his *(naughty girl, that's later)* ego and confirm his manly suspicion that he truly does look exactly like Brad Pitt when he smiles.

Beyond being blessedly easy to flatter, men also seem to have healthier egos than your average Jane. Even the balding man at the newsagents who always smells like last week's fish fry-up secretly believes that Don Juan has nothing on him. He would just appreciate it if women would mention it more often.

Men also think that they are interesting. Let him prattle on about whatever diesel/sports/money market/banking/household pet issue is consuming his interest at that moment, being careful occasionally to pout or form your mouth into a luscious 'O' while opening your eyes really big and speculating about what Superman would be like in bed. Needless to say, you need only regard this last paragraph if you're thinking sexy chat-up. For more general date-type chat-up, considering The Man Of Steel's sexual preferences at this stage is a very grim sign.

Oh, one last thing about the male psyche. It is all a lie. They aren't really this secure, at least most of them aren't. It seems to them terribly girly to be vulnerable or sensitive, particularly about something so central to them as their ego. Be gentle. Don't say anything really cruel except in jest. They won't take it well and, unlike us, won't be able to find any girlfriends afterwards to discuss it with over a box of tissues and some *Haagen Daz*.

If you have been checking out a particular chap over a period of time, are in possession of a good nose and are familiar with his scent, pick up a small bottle of it and dab a little on like perfume. If he's the least bit narcissistic or insecure (he's a man, so take it for granted) he won't even notice the scent, but will recognise that there is something really special about you, he's just not quite sure what it is. For you sex queens out there (and every woman is a potential sex queen) dab a little of your essence on your neck and wrists. Sounds nasty, I know, but it works. And it doesn't really smell like fish. It's nature's own little aphrodisiac. Exploit it. If you do decide to wear a scent of one sort or the other, apply it sparingly. Make sure that he will be required to stand close to appreciate it fully.

If you want to be really slick, try copying his breathing patterns. It's a great intimacy builder and he won't even know you're doing it.

To really slaughter the poor lamb, mirror his speaking style. If he repeatedly uses the word *look* or *listen* or *feel*, follow suit. You see, everybody fits into the category of being either visual, auditory or kinaesthetic. As we are far more likely to be attracted to someone on the same wavelength as us, the closer you can be to even the most superficial aspects of his being, the better.

Chemistry

Funnily enough, chemistry really does play an important part in seduction. When you're in love, or living with its down-market cousin lust, your body puts out phenylethylamine, dopamine and norepinephrine, leading to feelings of euphoria and well being similar to an amphetamine rush. After you're hooked, your body throws in its own ready made Valium, hence the sense of imminent well being. Post orgasm the body releases vasopressin and oxytocin, bonding you to your partner chemically.

This feeling can also be produced by eating large quantities of Belgian chocolates. The choice is yours.

Positive Thinking and Self Confidence

This is the primary tool used in turning an otherwise reasonable human being into a quivering mass of jelly, oozing at your feet, begging you to let them feed you peeled grapes.

There seems to be some assumption that to get a man's attention you have to be drop-dead gorgeous, or at least in the top ten, with say, Samantha Fox being an eleven. This is a sad lie produced by your own sorry mind to excuse the fact that there isn't currently a single person on this earth who is going to complain if you eat crackers in bed whilst reading a Mills and Boon.

Attractiveness is all in your head, I kid you not. Forget the fact that you have a bottom like the back side of a bus and breasts like infected bug bites. Ignore that your hairdresser thought that plum would be a good colour to put on your shiny chestnut hair and that you inherited most of your clothing from your cousin, who is a size three Metallica groupie. It doesn't matter, honest.

Nope, what counts here is that you think you are the sexiest, most desirable vixen your sad little town has ever seen.

Here's a test. Next time you're headed downtown for lunch, let that little fantasy float through your head. You know, the one about the ride-em lawn mower, or the one where your milkman's float breaks down and he needs to use the phone, but all you're wearing is that transparent blue nightie your best friend gave you as a gag gift on your last birthday. It makes you stand a little taller. You stick out your chest a little further than you usually would. You get a tricky little smile on your face that just won't go away. Men smile back, sometimes winking, other times nudging their friends, turning to stare after you. It works even better if you're not wearing any underwear. Come to think of it, it works pretty well when you're completely naked.

Be positive. Don't think about cellulite or, if you must, think about how great Ruben thought it was, or about how if you look really closely, Pamela Anderson also has cellulite and a pot belly, as do almost all of the women on this planet who are primarily valued within society for their appearance. Truth be known, 80% of women have cellulite. Doesn't it strike you as even a little odd that the stiletto trodden thighs and hips look should be considered an aberration?

Everyone looks different and every man likes something different. Don't sell yourself short by thinking that a man will not like you because you are a certain way. No doubt this can be true. But for every man who doesn't like that particular thing or that smorgasbord of cosmetic *faux pas*, there is bound to be a fella who disagrees with him. Even if there isn't, is that really the important thing? No. Remember, you're first. Worry primarily about how you feel about you. If you don't like something, change it, but don't change it just because someone else doesn't like it.

Before you go under that scalpel or start in on a tasty diet of ice cubes and sunflower seeds, try learning to accept your differences rather than condemning them.

Image

Well, there are some basic good ideas you should consider whilst you're grotting yourself up for Saturday night. You may be able to attract a swarm of pheromone-oozing men just by being a 'mega sex', but the type of man you end up chatting to will be largely determined by how you present yourself.

These tips will give you basic guidelines for a basic guy. You may be worrying that the better you look the more intimidating you will be. Stop it, this isn't a bad thing, you're just getting rid of the rotten apples before they spoil the barrel.

There are lots of tortuous things that you can do to con a man into slack-jawed, tight-trousered lust. Some are sly and others even your maiden aunt with her *close friend* Pat and thirty tomcats would know.

- Always define your waist. It doesn't really matter if you're six stone or sixteen, flaunt your waistline. If you don't have one, fake it with a thick black belt or something equally creative. Just make sure that there is a noticeable difference between your hip and waist ratio. Apparently the ideal waist has a ratio of 0:7. Once again, it's the whole fertility thing. A pre-pubescent girl or one who is going through the early stages of puberty will only have a very small hip-to-waist ratio. A woman who has passed through menopause has a thickened waist, lowering her ratio back down to pre-adolescence figures. Ironic, eh?

• While you're busy de-emphasising your waist, tuck some extra padding in your bra. The larger the bust line the less your waist is emphasised anyway. Come to think of it, large breasts seem to de-emphasise everything in life to the simplest of terms for men. My closest married male friend still greets me 'How are you, both of you?' I can only assume that his mother didn't breast feed or he was weaned too early.

• Regardless of the current fashion, stay away from heavy make-up. Wear the sheerest of foundations or he'll know that he's seeing your make-up, not your face. Need I remind you of all the man trouble Daryl Hannah had in *Blade Runner*?

• Dilated pupils are associated with sexual arousal. In previous centuries, young senoritas put drops of orange juice in their eyes to make their pupils dilate. Think about how it feels when you're peeling an orange with a hang nail. Yeah. In the sixties there were large quantities of pot around. In the eighties you could buy magnifying contacts (you still can, but then, you can also buy violet lenses. Need I say more?) For now your best bet is a little black eyeliner applied discreetly. Or stand in a dark room. Only Cher has my whole-hearted consent to wear gobs of black gook. I bet she's relieved.

- Always wear lipstick and blusher. Your lips and cheeks flush when you're aroused. Scarlett O'Hara bit her lips and pinched her cheeks and she got to take Rhett Butler home.

- Think healthy-looking when caring for your skin and hair. If these bits look well the rest of you is more likely to be healthy, and fruitful to boot.

- Find one look that makes you feel incredibly attractive and stick with it. Ideally, you should feel able to take over the world whilst wearing that red lycra number cut down to South Africa.

- Think about the impression you want to make, keeping in mind which kind of chatting-up you're attempting. If you are trying sexy *shmoozing*, look the part. Most men love the idea, if not the reality, of a one night stand. So, don't be girly or cute or wear floral patterns or track suits. Look as though you do it.

If you want him to call after the requisite three days, or if you want his phone number for a similar purpose, look like yourself. That's who you want him to want.

That's about it. Don't go on about your thighs or how your wardrobe is totally devoid of anything resembling a bold fashion statement. Men don't notice these things and only catty cows are evil enough to mention it. If they are the ones you are trying to impress, you're reading the wrong book.

Part of being a woman who steams up car windows while sitting in a convertible is being hated by those less generous members of the sisterhood. Be bigger than that.

Alcohol

Yes, we all know that one of the fastest ways to make yourself (with the exception of your bladder) more comfortable is to have a nip of something other than diet coke. Though if you're on a budget, a 2 litre bottle of the stuff can get you almost as silly as a six pack of lager, *sans* the hangover.

The major decision that has to be made here is in relation to quantity. If you're trying sexy chat-up, go ahead, another vodka won't affect your chances. Everybody's easier when they're intoxicated to the point of blindness. You're bound to run into somebody generous enough to take advantage of your inebriated state.

Remember, you may find yourself less inhibited when drunk, but the line between uninhibited and stupid is a very fine one. Bring along a nice friend with good taste to tell you when you've crossed the border. If your friend is also a bit drunk, this shouldn't be a problem for them.

Drunken behaviour does have its limits. After the age of twenty one you are expected to have some kind of self control. This age limit goes up if you're in America, as you are not allowed to buy alcohol until this age.

Driving whilst drunk is always unacceptable. There was a time when it was considered wild and wonderful to risk all in a fast car at two in the morning with half a bottle of Southern Comfort snuggled against your crotch, but thankfully those days are long over, raising your potential lifespan enormously. Never get so pissed that you can't see the logic of this.

If you want to impress somebody, a minimal amount of alcohol will suffice, thanks. No man wants to think that he may have to start going to the gym just so he can carry you home every Saturday night.

Another good thing about drinking is that you are liable to become a bit flushed when you have some ethanol chasing through your system. As previously mentioned, blushing is closely associated with sexual arousal. This adds a whole new dimension to why people go to warm places for sex holidays and why the gym has become such a popular chat-up joint.

Telephoning

If you fancy someone it is always possible to get their phone number, unless they happen to be famous, in which case it is still possible, just more expensive.

Once you have this grail, the question is what to do with it. The obvious answer is to place your fingers on the buttons and dial whilst the receiver is held to your ear. Believe me, it's ten times easier to do this than actually to walk up to somebody and say something intelligent and witty while mimicking their breathing and speech patterns, pouting your lips and holding in the requisite lager belch (assuming that you were paying attention to the *Alcohol* chapter).

It is critical that you establish who you are and where you met before you embark on any serious chatting-up. Never say 'Hi, it's me' until you're married, unless you've got a really distinctive speech impediment, like say, an American accent.

I know you have to agonise over what you are going to say before you say it. Silly really, no matter what you say, at some point they're going to pick up on the fact that you're not calling to sell them double glazing. Because I know that last sentence was less than 100% helpful, here are some good basics that aren't quite as flinch-worthy as 'Hi-don't-yell-at-me-do-you-want-to-go-out?'

If you have spoken to this person before and actually got the number from him, your range of lines is far broader.

- Hi, it's ____, I met you at ____, I was just sorting out my purse/ washing my trousers/skirt/red lace crotchless panties and I found your number.

- Hey, this is ____, I'm watching *Top Gear* and I thought I'd better ring you to make sure you're tuned in because they are doing a feature on the Datsun/Nissan Z series cars and they have the bit in there about how the electricals in the 1978 280Z were a real problem, like I was saying last week, and seeing as how you didn't believe me and wanted to buy one, I thought I should call and gloat.

Obviously this one has many highly variable combinations. You don't always have to be calling to gloat, but since you are already putting him in a position of power by calling, you may find yourself feeling a bit more secure if you can get a little bit of an upper hand in the beginning of the conversation.

- Hello, ____ here. My date for tonight just called to say that he's married an exotic dancer and run off to Las Vegas for the honeymoon and I was thinking maybe you might like to buy me a chocolate milkshake to console me.

Once again, you can alter it a bit. Have a sense of the dramatic and ensure that he has a good sense of humour if you are actually going to say the above, verbatim.

- Yo, it's ____, my room mate and I were arguing about whether Man Ray is considered the father of Da Daism or if he was simply a prominent member of the movement, and I remembered that you read Art at Oxford and thought you may have some insights into the matter.

Change as appropriate.

'Blind calling' someone is different. If you obtained the number through a friend or whatever, you haven't been invited. Usually it's flattering enough that they won't be horrible about it, so don't worry too much.

Your approach:

- Hi, you might remember me from ____, it's ____. I got your number from ____. I hope you don't mind.(pause) Two tickets to ____ just landed in my lap and I thought you might want to join me.

If he happens to turn you down, be grateful that he can't see your expression through the phone lines. Act smart and perky as if it doesn't really matter to you, because you've got about twenty guys on the line and you just thought you'd make his sorry existence a little brighter by taking him out for some fun. Leave a number and let him call next time.

Something to remember if you are calling a guy: men have this twisted view that if you call them you are somehow dependent and needy. This is moronic. If we were weak and whiny we would be expecting them to make all of the moves. Calling a man takes a lot of courage, and the independence to look past the norms and expectations of society. It takes strength of character, or at least a good shot of whiskey. If he can't see that, he's not worth the space he's taking up on this planet and certainly doesn't deserve you.

Where To Go On A Date

A not very wise but mighty sexy man once told me following our first date to the cinema, 'Never go out with a guy if he wants to take you to the cinema for your first date. It means that he is only interested in one thing, and it isn't conversation.' Important safety tip.

Best bet for a first date is to make it during the daylight hours. Go out to lunch during a weekday if your workplaces are close and you're not terribly busy. If that fails, go for a picnic or a leisurely stroll on a Sunday afternoon. This works best if you have a dog. If there is an uncomfortable pause in conversation, you can always start fussing with your canine. If you just want to kick around in the sheets with him for a spell, ignore this paragraph.

You may have something in your life that is really important to you in which he has some vague interest. If you spend most of your free time compiling the works of prominent anthropologists into one clear and decisive theory concerning the extinction of Homo Sapiens Neanderthalis, then by all means take him down to the Natural History Museum and explain the basics of what you're dealing with. If he is really interested in you he will welcome this chance to get such an intimate insight into how your mind works. Nice thing too; if you're talking about your obsession, you are unlikely to run out of things to say.

Avoid nocturnal activities for your first outing. Night dates usually have sexual overtones, and you may feel pressured by this. Even if you have a goodbye kiss on your first daytime date, it doesn't have to have sexual overtones. After a night out you know that the first place the person is headed is either the shower or bed. With a day date you could be headed almost anywhere, and are probably expected there at a certain time. The exception to this is going out for a casual drink. You can't move directly from the pub to the bed without feeling as though you have missed an essential step, like opening the front door.

Handling The First Date

Funny thing about dating, no matter how keen you are, you're not allowed to show it. You both know it. You both thought about your attire for more than twenty seconds, you both brushed your teeth twice before you met, and still you have to be cool. So be cool.

Think carefully about your clothing. You may look your utter best in that rubber catsuit with the crotch zipper, but it's not what you want to show up in for a drink in a quiet little neighbourhood pub. I know, it's really tempting to overdress, but don't. It's always better to underdress than overdress. If you wear an evening dress to a picnic it looks like you're trying too hard. If you wear jeans and a t-shirt to a cocktail party, it makes you look confident and *devil-may-care*. Act as though you don't even notice that you're dressed worse than the servers and all men will worship you, even if they do suspect that you're a bit of rough.

My worst date ever was at Disneyland. It was a first date and as we pulled in to meet Mickey and Minnie, he slapped me. Not nice. Anyway, I was about an hour away from home and didn't have enough money for a cab. We left Goofy and pals to their own devices after only an hour because I was so uncomfortable, yet the guy still insisted on finding awful things to do until ten that evening (including walking through a shopping centre, announcing at the top of his voice that my breasts weren't as large as he would like them to be). All of this could have been avoided had I followed my roommate's advice that we take my car, so that if I got into an uncomfortable, volatile or potentially dangerous situation, I'd have a means of escape. Needless to say, my petrol bills have gone up since.

Besides being an immediate exit, should you for some reason feel uncomfortable with a guy and not want to see him again, you sure as hell don't want him to know where you live. If you haven't a car, discuss a meeting place close to a bus station.

Unless you're taking public transport and your bus only goes every half hour or so, make a point of being a little late. Not dramatically late, but a little. Ten minutes of clock watching will be good for him. Builds character. Do come bearing profuse apologies, however. It's rude not to. Remember, you're being cool.

You might be one of those people who has a really easy time talking to men. You might not. Remember how hard you worked to establish that you are the sexiest thing your sad little town has ever seen and start to flirt. Smile a lot and make him feel like he is equally desirable. As mentioned, most guys want to think you think this anyway, and they'll be glad you mentioned it. Don't worry about lapses in conversation. You're getting to know each other. By all means feel free to ask him another question about his hobby of underwater basket weaving.

Things to talk about:

- Talk about your days. Just because he's not an old friend doesn't mean you can't treat him like one

- Basic statistics; brothers and sisters, education, children

- Books and movies

- Hobbies

If you can't think of anything else to talk about after you have made it through this list, it's probably best just to let it go. Be glad you brought your own car.

With the price of cellular phones today and the minimal service charges, there is really no reason why you, a single girl, shouldn't have one. They are an essential safety accessory, not to mention being an excellent tool for getting out of a less than ideal dating situation.

If you are not really sure about the man you're going out with, or even as a general safety precaution, have a friend call you at an appointed time. This way if things are going really badly you can always pretend the call is a dire emergency and make your exit.

In contrast, if things are going really well, you may decide that you want to invite the guy back to your place. If you do so, be sure that you trust the man and are fully aware of the sexual suggestiveness in your offer. On a practical level, get your blood stained panties out of the sink and clean under the seat of the toilet. Clear the pictures of your *ex* off the bedside table.

Always remember, even if you decide to invite a man into your lair, this does not automatically mean you have to get physical with him. Don't let him pretend that it does. Unless it does.

On a final note, let the man know you are having a good time if you are. Even if they don't fancy you so much after all, they want to know that they are doing the right thing and are able to show a girl a good time.

Impressing

The kind of man you're looking for will be impressed just by the fact that you are making the effort to chat him up.

As a general rule, however tempting it may be, do not go out of your way to impress a man. It won't work. The idea is that if you feel the need to talk about all of the really amazing things that you have said, done, felt or met over the years, you are actually only trying to camouflage a very boring, insecure and otherwise unattractive person within yourself.

You can drop all the names you want, but if they are dating you because you know someone who can get Claudia Schiffer's E Mail number, you'll find it a less than perfect base for a relationship and you shouldn't be too surprised if you can't find much to say to each other after that.

Be yourself. If that doesn't impress him there isn't a lot of point in trying to get any further.

One more thing. If you are a powerful woman, don't you dare downplay it. I don't care if men are intimidated by you, I don't care how difficult it is to find a date. Do not pretend that you are not powerful. Men need to learn just how strong women can be, and they are never going to figure it out if you are going to simper and defer to him because he has a penis. Things don't change simply because you want them to. Things change because you make them change. I believe in gang violence and I know where you live. That's a lie, but you get the idea. I'm not asking you to do this for womankind. That's entirely too altruistic; do it for yourself. It takes a powerful man to be with a powerful woman. Haven't you dated enough inadequate men? Join the club, sister.

Talking

There is a saying that goes *you can catch more flies with honey than with vinegar.* This is a lie. Maybe it is all part of their hunting instinct, but there is nothing that seems to keep a man sniffing about your skirts longer than being really mean to him. Go ahead, it's fun to tease, be a little cruel, push him away. Just be sure to smile and show your dimples while you're doing it.

You will run into the occasional man with whom this will not work, but only rarely. It is from this persistence of attention in the face of complete and utter failure that I have drawn the conclusion that all men are essentially romantics.

Romance is drama, action. Take a man out and what does he want to see? Action flicks. He doesn't want to see romances. Romance is soft and boring and not nearly as interesting as blood and guts and cannibalistic aliens. However, when it comes to actual real life contact with females they want that extra element of drama. When love is involved they don't want it to be easy, they want that bit of melodrama, much the same as when at the movies they want to see exploding brains instead of kissing for that added zing.

That's romance. How unromantic.

Another aspect of this has to do with getting the best
cave girl into his lair. The harder she is to get and the
more competition there is with other men, the more
worthwhile she is apt to be. I am not a proponent of
game playing, particularly 'hard to get', but in recent
years, months, days it has come to my attention that
this seems to be the best way to get and keep attention.
You have to have strong nerves, a quick brain and
the subtlety of a water buffalo. That doesn't mean
I'm recommending this particular course of action. If
you start telling lies during courtship, what hope is
there for any future relationship? Besides, there are
guys out there who will run at any whiff of game
playing. There are others who will assume that you
aren't playing games at all, you just don't like their
smell.

Decide which type of man you have, Mr. Sensitive
who will assume you're passing him 'go away' hints
if you walk past his desk without a friendly smile, or
Fred Flintstone who is out chasing any skirt who has
the good sense to say no. Maturity level is usually a
good indicator. If he strikes you as dreadfully boyish,
he probably would like to play a few childish games
before you move onto anything as sensible as dinner.
Older men respect the value of time and won't torture
you with moronic behaviour.

I guess the real question is then, 'do you want a man
who is going to take up all of your time playing jump
rope or do you want the security of somebody who
knows what they want and respects your needs?' I

know, there is a double-dutcher in all of us, and a masochist to boot. The initial rushes of adrenaline can be very exhilarating. They can also be incredibly painful. Keep your fingers out of this fire.

Somebody once came up with the idea that if you concentrate exclusively on the other person, at least for the first couple of meetings, some wonderful, magical things will happen and the person you are with will come to believe that you are not a nosy negative-personality git, but a sensitive, caring person who finds her date completely fascinating.

This is silly. Try to talk naturally. Yes, it's lovely if you can at least make an effort to give a thought to the person across the table from you, but do try to give yourself equal floor space. There is something sexy about someone who is a little self-centred. Not a lot, but a little.

Never nag a man or make him feel he has done something foolish. He is not a child and will know if he has been naughty. You can gently remind him of something, but don't harp on or make him feel stupid about anything he may or may not have done. You'll find that he appreciates you and loves you much better for it.

If you came to him with a problem that you want to talk about, make it clear that it is not his fault and you are not trying to accuse him of anything. Make sure he understands that you may neither want nor expect him to find a solution for the problem. Both of these things will make your time together far more comfortable.

Bullshit

If you're on an actual date, not a pre-coital lust bath, be yourself. Don't even think about playing a part. There is little point to such artifice as you will start to resent any role you would be playing after a very short period of time, and there are bound to be cracks in your performance. Besides, he'll probably have you figured out by the time your second child is born.

Now, if you are wallowing in the bubbles of carnal desire , you can have a little more fun, particularly if you're in a foreign country.

I lived in Greece for a few months and during that time I tried at least one night of the week to con some poor olive oil gorged Adonis into believing that I was not just any loose knickered westerner, but a movie star who was over to visit a sister who was married to a Greek. It was a wonderful story that could be changed and embellished to suit any situation. The release schedule for Greece on American flicks is about nine months behind Britain and up to a year behind America, so I could conveniently pick a movie that was known but couldn't yet have been seen. Lots of drinks were bought for me, I was invited onto Bouzooki stages, and I parted company with dozens of Greeks bearing the promise that they would be sure to look for me in my up and coming release. I don't suggest trying this at your local.

Men speak

Men often don't understand the way that women talk, or they misinterpret what women are trying to express to them. Suppose your man is out of work and you want him to feel that you are supporting him completely in his efforts to find employment. Don't come up to him with the job vacancy ads insisting that this or that position is just perfect for him. Instead ask his opinion on the advertisement. This slight rephrasing could make the whole difference in how they react to you and your proposition.

It isn't a matter of saying or not saying something that you may or may not feel. It is a question of translating into their language.

Having said that, women are frequently accused of being horribly manipulative wenches with noses for trouble and a knack for saying what they mean without ever saying what they mean. The first man to make this accusation was obviously looking in the mirror. Recognise these?

- My family is a bit odd. (You're never meeting my family.)

- Let's go for a walk. (Let's go to the pub.)

- Maybe I can get started on it later. (If I leave it long enough, you'll get fed up and do it yourself.)

- Are there any crisps? (Get me some crisps.)

- You shouldn't drive all the way here, it's getting dark. (I don't want to see you.)

- I'm not sure I have enough petrol to get home. (Can I stay here?)

- Haven't you already seen this? (Oh God, another girly flick.)

- I like a woman who doesn't spend too much time on her appearance. (I want a natural beauty.)

So we all do it.

Sense Of Humour

Never underestimate the sexiness of a sense of humour. A sense of humour implies a silliness, a connection with the inner child and a freedom from inhibitions that can be devastatingly attractive, though it can be painfully intimidating. Remember what Jessica Rabbit said in *Who Framed Roger Rabbit?* when somebody asked her why she married Roger: 'He makes me laugh.'

If you don't have a sense of humour either get one or get used to your role in life as a straight (wo)man; the position from which you don't get to say anything amusing yourself but must be well behaved whilst someone is funny at your expense.

If you do happen to be a funny person, don't get so carried away that your chat-up is suddenly a stand up routine. That's intimidating and often moves quickly towards embarrassment. If he's not funny, don't laugh at his jokes. You would be doing anybody with whom he has future contact a great disservice.

All variations on singledom require a sense of humour. Never approach a potential conquest with a backhanded complement without being supremely confident of the nature of their humour or the effect of your dimples. Don't approach someone who is dancing in a disco with the line 'you have a beautiful body, but have no idea how to move it, let me teach you,' and expect them to have the sense of humour to allow them not to physically assault you.

You will also function much better in a relationship if you have the ability to laugh at yourself and look at everything with a sense of humour. There is no need for straight laced seriousness. Nervous breakdowns aren't healthy and tend to make a very poor bonding compound.

Body Language - Reading and Sending The Signs

Body language is ever so useful. It is the primary tool used to indicate that your hormones have just kicked into overdrive. It can also give excellent *piss off* signals. Your body articulates everything without you having to say anything. For our purposes, it is important that you have a good understanding of your body language as well as that of the fly you're trying to lure into your web.

The first thing to remember when trying to attract a man, or anybody really, is to keep your body language very open. That means no crossing of the arms. Keep your shoulders down. Keep your body relaxed and people will assume that you are relaxed. If you look tense people will think you are trying too hard. Always remember (even if you're pretending) that you are doing them a favour. Don't be scared.

After a bit of practice you may come to notice that when you fancy someone your foot has a funny tendency to point towards that person. The same compulsion may come over someone who fancies you. Nature's compass.

While we're on the subject, have you ever noticed that when a man is on the make, particularly if he sees a filly he'd fancy in his corral, he links his thumbs in his belt-loops like a cow hand out of a bad B-movie with his fingers pointing towards his nether regions? Well he does. And if he doesn't, it's likely that his hands are hidden away in a pocket somewhere, still pointing.

If you are holding something, particularly of a phallic nature, a nail file, a cocktail stirrer, a pen, or a vibrator, point it towards him. Apparently it has the same affect on men as their little *have you noticed that I have a penis, look, it's right here where I'm pointing* gesture is supposed to have on us.

Give him *The Look*. You know, the one where you stare at him until he notices and then look away briefly like you're shy. Then you look at him again, this time lingering three seconds beyond good manners and dropping your gaze down to his lips and then down to his trousers, whereupon you bite your lip and sigh and look back at his face, big eyed. Repeat this, or a variation on the theme for about five minutes, once every thirty seconds. One study found that this technique hooked 60% of men inside of ten minutes. If he ends up being far less juicy close up than he was across the room you can always say what Demi Moore said to Rob Lowe in *About Last Night*; 'I wasn't looking at you. The clock was above your head.'

Well, now you've tempted him from across the room. Don't stop with the eyes. O.K., you're too shy to stare at his face. Try making eye contact with just one of his eyes, and then focus on the other after a few minutes. It gives the illusion that you are looking deeply into his soul, when really you're just counting his eyelashes. Another recent study found that complete strangers who stare into each other's eyes for two minutes reported a passionate feeling akin to love after only a two-minute eye up.

Granted, all of this staring can be a little disconcerting. When you're in a conversation you may find it easiest to look into his eyes and then look away coquettishly. Give and then remove your attention. It all has to do with that little bit of tease. Don't forget how much they love the chase. While you're butterflying your lashes prettily, try to stand, at most, eighteen inches apart. Psychologists claim that the likelihood of two people who are standing this close having a sexual encounter is high.

Use any excuse to touch him. Physical contact breaks down far more barriers much more quickly than talking ever could. Touch his arm to emphasise a point. Grab his wrist to look at his watch. Imply familiarity and intimacy will follow.

Always smile and act interested. It doesn't really matter which bit you're interested in.

Teamwork

There are a number of ways to look at bringing a friend with you. No matter how much you love your best mate, if she is a man magnet and your lust legs haven't quite kicked in yet, leave her at home. There are women like this. I'm sure that you can think of at least one. They are always on the prowl and seem to work on men like a tonic. Until you have your relations with men worked out to the point where you are equally magnetic, might I recommend that you just leave her at home? The last thing your ego needs when you are trying to build up to a good chat-up is a thunder stealer.

On the other hand, when people go out in social situations it tends to be in pairs. If you can talk her into going for the dud your amour has dragged along for the evening, the situation, mathematically speaking, will be only half as embarrassing. Your call. Another nice thing about bringing a friend along is that you can entertain each other whilst waiting for Mr. Vaguely-Interesting to come along. Also, people tend to wonder what's wrong with your personal hygiene that you have to show up to social situations all by yourself.

Girlfriends are good for that sense of camaraderie. It won't be nearly so intimidating entering *Wally's Willy World* if you have a friend with you to help you take the piss out of all of those people by whom you may be feeling intimidated. If she is a really good pal she will also make a point of telling you that you look like an under-done potato if your fashion sense wasn't on full throttle when you were dressing. Be sure to make some ground rules first and you should be fine.

Targeting

Studies have shown that it is typically people of roughly equal attractiveness who will be together. Attractiveness isn't just the physical, it's the whole package. Personality, sense of humour, sex appeal, it all adds up. This sheds a little light on the whole ugly rock star/ beautiful supermodel phenomena, not that my catty self is thinking of anybody in particular, Mick and Rod.

Another thing that seems to attract people to each other is a certain similarity in appearance. Not necessarily colouring or features, but maybe basic body structure, build, ethnicity. In fact, this urge to merge with someone like yourself is so strong that studies have shown that relationships may actually last longer when this is a factor. Maybe it's narcissism or just being comfortable with something imminently familiar, but there seems to be something to it.

So, you are much more likely to score with a man if you live in a small town where there has been a lot of inbreeding. Short of that, look for someone who reminds you of you.

While we're here let's have a little chat about the different sorts of men, shall we?

Bad Boys:
Don't go for bad boys. This is intrinsically silly. First off, they're bad, secondly, they are boys. I shouldn't have to say any more than that, but obviously I must, as so many women still get all stupid and sloppy when a guy in leather oozes in their direction. You don't want a bad boy. They break your heart and steal your money and give you funny looking kids with long greasy hair and surly manners. They are childish in their attitudes towards both relationships and women. Since they don't have a healthy view of women, they treat them as if they are children, or worse, toys. Have some self-respect. Be a woman, not a doormat. Have the sense not to seek out men on purpose who will try to hurt you. It's not their fault or problem, it's yours. Think about how you feel about yourself if you torture yourself in this way. It's not healthy.

Don't ever think that he is going to change or that maybe he's not as naughty as all that. He won't and he is.

Where to find: Santa Pod on race day. He likes to smell the part.

The Blue Print Man:

If you tend to go for a certain type of man, stop it. This is silly and destructive. You can miss so many wonderful opportunities if you think only in terms of 'oh no, I don't want him, he's not my type.' My mum would date only blondes. My dad has black hair, and though they were good friends, nothing really came of it until they started rolling around on the carpet one Valentine's Day. They have been married for 26 years and counting. O.K., so she was a little shallow. That's the point. I'm not saying that you should start dating bums to break your habit of going out just with successful men, I'm only suggesting that maybe you don't want to write someone off because he weighs in below your requisite cut off of fourteen stone. Don't be so shallow. Think about all of those men of whom we are so fond because they love women, all women. Be one of the women who loves and finds something valuable in all men.

Where to find: Where did you find the last one?

Older men #1:
He is a silver haired fox. His cuffs are a bit frayed because his tailor is behind. He is taking you to a hotel because his house is being painted and he can't stand the fumes. He wonders if you would leave the tip because he hasn't any change. He often answers to the name of Willy Loman. BUT:

He's so sweet. He is so besotted with you and isn't it a shame that his wife died in that horrible car accident.

Funny how, if you fish around in his pocket you'll find that he still carries his wedding band in with his pocket knife and lint. Don't be stupid. Learn to read the signs. Never hesitate in asking yourself, 'Why, if this man is such a catch, is he single?'

Where to find: A single room at a two star bed and breakfast on a Wednesday.

Older men #2:
You tell him how much you love Italian food and he flies you to Italy for the evening. You pop in to the Army Navy with him to buy a pair of stockings, as his large bearded collie just tore yours to pieces, and you walk out with three stunning new outfits, mostly in pale colours.

He gets inexplicably angry when you do something irresponsible. When you accomplish something wonderful he couldn't be more proud if he had done it himself. He talks easily of the mother of his children, whether he is married to her or not.

You seem to be working on some kind of a point system with him. The longer you stay and the more charming the things you do, the better the prizes get. Make no mistake, the prizes are wonderful. Houses, vacations, silks, cars, pink poodles.

They are slick and it does happen quickly. One minute you're happily working a dead end job in the local saw mill and the next you are out of work in your flat in Morocco with a man who thinks the sun rises and sets in your knickers and only pesters you on weekends. Oh sure, you say, what's the downside?

It may not sound relevant now, but you will never have his heart. You are a toy, and as such can be broken and cast aside thoughtlessly and without recourse. Your mum will be really embarrassed.

Where to find: Hard to say. Most urban areas will have a handful of sugar daddies on the prowl. Look glamorous and hang around tall buildings.

Older Men #3:
These are the good ones, the grown-ups. Yes, their marriage dissolved, no he didn't get custody of the children, but he sees them every weekend and pays child support.

He is responsible and won't play stupid games to win your heart. He will be honest. A rare man indeed.

This is the guy you search for after you have gone out with all of those rude young men with baggy jeans and bad attitudes. Their *abs* aren't as firm and the miles show in the lines around their eyes, but he makes no excuses and keeps his promises. He will never treat you mean to keep you keen.

Where to find: I'll tell you for another fiver.

Younger men:
They want so much to grow up. Their hormones are raging and the second time you have sex he sprays all over your thigh. The first time he was impotent. The sex is the good part.

The bad part is that you pay for everything, there is only a future in it if you want to start breast feeding, and there isn't a chance in hell of you getting along with each other's friends.

So it's pretty much like most guys, but with worse skin.

Where to find: Outside the pub on Saturday night, acting casual.

Bimboys:
There is a wonderful Los Angeles anthem of a sort
that goes 'I like 'em big and *stupid*, I like them big and
real *dumb*.' It continues on with charming images like
Superman with a lobotomy etc., but you get the idea.

They're great. Their only two passions in life, that
they remember anyway, are you and football. Or you
and Nintendo. Or you and beer. Beware, if you are
out of their immediate sight line they may forget that
you are one of the two passions that they are capable
of processing in those little acorns they call brains.

They are so pretty and well toned. They are very
secure because they are not bright enough to feel
threatened, and won't see anything at all wrong with
your being a powerful woman. They aren't the least
bit demanding. Just make sure always to keep your
tongue in his mouth to stop him from talking.

Where to find: Lost in the frozen fish section at Tesco.

Jocks:
Similar to bimboys in that they have room for only
two passions; the press and their sport. Sometimes
you can slip in during the off season. These aren't
bad guys, they might even have brains. It's just that
they are never expected to use them.

They do have lovely tight bottoms, but if you become
a player's wife you have to do embarrassing interviews

for GMTV when your man's team wins to find out if you're thrilled or not.

Where to find: The locker room. It takes a brave heart and a strong stomach.

Nerds:

The nice thing about nerds, some of them anyway, is that they learned to stop taking themselves so seriously around the time they hit university. By the time they finish their doctorate in physics at Cambridge, they are the life of the party. Stupid looking guys make up for their shortcomings with other assets. They are funny, witty, sweet and really good in bed. They spent that A level in celibacy reading some very racy books and remembered all they read. They are worth it.

Where to find: The law library or behind a very large desk in a corner office.

Colleagues:

If you are a grown up, this is fine. Yup, if you are totally cool with getting on with them after they have dumped you and done a war dance on your heart, go ahead. If you think that you can walk past his desk without playing with that funny little bit of hair at the back of his neck, sure. If the two of you can refrain from doing it on the copier at lunch, O.K. . . . Liar.

Where to find them: Most of the cute ones hang out in advertising.

Wolves:

This is the man with the wife and children who still dates. He has found his perfect match and is happy with his choice, as long as she isn't the only choice. He likes to play the field. His extra-marital affairs may never lead to actual sex; he mostly likes to know that he could if he wanted to. On one level or another his behaviour is rooted in insecurity. He may feel that his beloved is too good for him (seems likely), that he is unattractive or he could even have repressed homosexual tendencies he is trying to mask in real or assumed sexual relations. He may never learn to recognise his pattern, but you should.

Where to find: At the theatre with one hand holding his wife's hand and the other a stranger's bum.

Pigs:

The pig works on a cycle of highly erratic serial monogamy. For two or three years he will want stay in a relationship and be a doting lover. He may even want to marry you. Then all of the sudden he wants to be free and stay free and thinks that he may never want to be monogamous again. He may even be enough of an egotist to think that the woman he has rejected will just sit and wait on the off-chance that he will come back to her. Then somebody else sweeps him off his feet and he wants to be back at the beginning of the cycle. He will be shocked at each of the many hearts he breaks. Eventually he will end up a fat alcoholic with three kids on child support, but he will still think himself a sex god even after all of the perks have dried up. Best avoided: notice all of the times that *he wants* was mentioned in this paragraph. He is a petulant, insecure child. You need a man.

Where to find: There is one of these in every man. The trick is in how well they can control it.

Construction Workers:
I'm sure that there are some really wonderful construction workers out there with the hearts of poets and the thighs of Sylvester Stallone. Unfortunately most of the ones that I run into have big old beer bellies and consider the height of polite conversation to be 'Oi, nice beaver'. Construction workers do not say all of these things in order to pick us up. They say these things because they are harassing us. Fight back, they won't do anything. Point out that they are harassing you and that there is no excuse whatsoever for that kind of behaviour. Don't just take it. Aren't you tired of having to cringe every time you walk past a building site?

Where to find: Don't make me tell you.

Safe Men:
Also known as the transition or rebound man, he's a really swell guy. There is not a thing in the world wrong with him. He's a little slow, he doesn't achieve

much, but he's got steady work. He likes kids and adores you. He is very . . . boring. The sparks of passion may not fly, but they are not the least bit likely to hurt you. Such men are, if nothing else, reliable. Many girls end up marrying these men. Some end up happy with this situation. Most of us turn over and start snoring loudly. Safe men are good for patching up a broken heart, but in terms of forever, they're a little slice of purgatory.

Where to find: At exactly the same spot, at precisely the same time in the same train yard they have been going to since they were a kid.

Gay Men:
Ah, the ultimate safe man. Can't get into trouble with this one, you think. Think again.

There are two types of gay men. The only difference between these two types is how they're doing with storage space. The first type is in the closet. He may have realised very early in life that his sexual preference is not entirely acceptable to a great deal of society and shoves it as much as possible out of the view of others. He may even get married and have a family, but shams like this rarely last a lifetime and can be truly horrible for the person who was unwittingly used in the exchange as a cover.

The second type of gay man is doing well in the area of clothing storage. He knows he's gay, you know it.

You may still fall in love. The only problem is that he will love you as a friend, maybe even as a best friend, maybe as a wife, but not in the biblical sense. This can be very painful for both parties because what is cannot be changed. It's best to be friends and keep the score very much in mind. They can be the best girlfriends you will ever have.

Where to find: 10% of the population is gay. If you think you don't know any gay people, check your premises.

Remember that it is alright if you screw up and target the wrong men. God isn't keeping a score card on you. If you do it consistently, however, you might want to start reconsidering some of your choices. It's all a learning experience.

Sex

If God wanted us to take sex seriously, the slapping of two stomachs together wouldn't sound like cow farts. Penis' wouldn't look like plucked turkey necks. Banana flavoured condoms would never have been invented. Nipples wouldn't turn inside out and ladies would never fart. It most certainly wouldn't be so messy.

It is easy to look at sex too soberly. You are at your most vulnerable when you are naked. You are exposing all of those bits about which you feel most self-conscious. Sex for women is so often associated with emotion, you are giving some of that away too.

It's scary, I know. Act like a grown up. Be honest about it. If you're having a hard time with it emotionally or physically, tell your partner. If you have reached the point where you can expose so much of yourself physically, surely you can open a few emotional windows.

Remember all of the work that you did previously to overcome being obsessed with the idea that your physical appearance could be the only lure. Don't suddenly become shy and self conscious about your body just because there doesn't happen to be a great deal covering it. When you say things like, 'don't turn on the lights, I have horrible thighs' you are breaking down the established intimacy and sexiness you had previously. Confidence and a *devil-may-care* attitude are the key.

Most men are too nice to say it, because they know how important it is to us when we are at our most vulnerable, but they hate pillow talk. An orgasm takes a lot more out of a man then it does a woman. As I hope you already know, we can go for days and days of multiple orgasms and find that each one energises and relaxes us, but it simply isn't the same for a man. He gets tired and doesn't want to give you much more than a drooly cuddle, if that. Be kind, have your intimate conversations in the morning after waking him up with some orange juice and coffee. He'll thank you for it later. The same goes for repeat performances.

Always be enthusiastic. If he is doing something wrong, gently correct him. Don't just lie there and take it, scratch his back, bite his ears, thrust that pelvis. You don't have to be a walking Kama Sutra, but take some initiative. Don't ever act like you're doing him a favour by lying under your mirrored ceiling. Act as if he's doing you a huge favour, even if he isn't.

Don't get too huffy about impotence. It isn't personal, it has nothing to do with you. Most men experience first night impotence at one time or another in their lives. This is O.K.. Don't try to force it. If it really isn't working out for him, invite him simply to sleep with you for the night. If he wakes up with his little buddy in a better mood, fine. This is particularly a problem with older men. Look out for it.

Don't allow yourself to be pressured into sexual relations. Be sure that it is exactly what you want to do. If possible, plan it. You'll feel better in the morning. Spontaneous sexual relations outside of a relationship can be confusing and painful. If you really fancy someone and don't think that you could handle sharing, make that clear from the very beginning. Don't have sex with someone assuming that this will be the twine that will keep him tied to your skirt strings. Base your relationships on emotions, not bodily fluids.

It is important to remember that not every lover wants the same thing. In fact, if they are brutally honest and blatantly uninhibited, you'll find that each and every lover you have will be sexually different. If you've got more than one fish on the line, be careful to remember who likes what. It would be really embarrassing if you started playing dominatrix with the wrong man.

Don't laugh and point.

Oh sure, I know that you want to. Honest person that I am I actually did that once. It was funny at the time, but it became seriously unfunny during the nine month dry spell that followed. So, as much as I enjoy promoting penile anxiety, I abstain from such activities now.

One of my Nans maintains that you should never let a man see you naked. She claims that my long suffering grandfather never saw her naked because she always kept on at least one knee high stocking when crawling into bed. The mind boggles. This is probably taking it all a little far, but there is something in the idea that you can look more naked when you have on a few scraps of clothing.

Someone who was probably really famous and way more important than me once said that the mind is the main erogenous zone. Probably so. There is a pretty sizable difference between having an orgasm and having a great orgasm. For most people this difference can be found in two different ways: either be in love; or make love in a different way. *Vive la difference* if you have both.

Orgasms

After the arousal phase, which for most women lasts about fifteen minutes to half an hour, you may, with the help of the right toy or man (batteries not included) meet your own big 'O'.

Only 30% of women come through vaginal penetration. Truth be known, there are about three different types of female orgasms possible. The first and most man friendly is the vaginal orgasm which, as previously mentioned, only happens about 30% of the time. The second type is the clitoral orgasm, the most woman friendly. Many women, however, do find that their clitoris is entirely too sensitive for this kind of attention and prefer vaginal stimulation (indirect clitoral stimulation through the connective tissues) or the third type of orgasm. This is the type that allows women to come in alleyways and on top of the work tops. It is as rapid as a man's but usually cannot be achieved after too much clitoral stimulation. Don't feel bad if this does not work for you, it doesn't for everybody.

What happens is this: deep penetration can stimulate the peritoneum (the sensitive lining of the abdominal cavity), leading sometimes to an even more intense but definitely different sort of orgasm. It is very satisfying and, whilst it is not a necessary reaction for a sex queen to have, it certainly doesn't hurt.

All this being said, it appears that the most sure-fire way to an orgasm is through clitoral stimulation, direct or indirect. So why is it placed in such an inaccessible spot? Well of course I have an explanation. We have a clitoris for the same reason that men have nipples.

The human foetus is essentially identical regarding the first little bit for both male and female. In a male embryo, after a spell, that nasty little Y chromosome kicks in, releasing hormones and causing the foetus to evolve male genitalia. The female foetus continues as before. Now, before the start of the hormonal buelabase, the nipples and primary genitalia (clits and dicks) had already begun to form. This is made evident in man's completely useless nipples and a woman's clitoris. That's right. Men's nipples are baby breasts and women's clits are very small penis' with no more evolutionary significance than male tits. Depressing but true.

Contraception

Always practice safe sex. Don't think for a minute that being 'straight' or a non drug-user is going to keep you from getting any one of the multiple gooey monsters that attack the unsuspecting naughty person's genitals. The only way to keep yourself absolutely safe is to abstain from all sexual contact, male or female and move to an armed convent.

Condoms

Short of militant measures, always wear a condom, preferably in conjunction with a spermicidal cream, lotion, gel or foam that contains nonoxidal No.9. This also applies to oral sex. A word of warning, regular condoms taste really bad and with spermicide, and even some plain old lubricants, will act like a short term novacaine and turn your mouth numb. Use flavoured condoms. Mouth guards are sometimes available for men free from any health care clinic, for blokes worth their salt who think that twats are beautiful.

Never use an oil based lubricant in conjunction with a condom, this includes massage oil, much of which is based on the oil in soy beans. Always stick with water based lubricants such as K-Y Jelly and Astra Glide. If you have a regular problem with lubrication either check with your GP for a hormonal imbalance or get yourself a new man.

Female Condoms

Well, you don't have to leave it to the man, which is a good thing. If you are one of the 70% of women who is unable to achieve an orgasm through intercourse, the little ring that bumps your clit might be just the thing. Unlike the traditional male condom it can be applied even before you leave your bathroom. But it looks and sounds like a plastic bag. It is horrendously expensive, though you can get them free now from family planning clinics.

Diaphragms and Cervical Caps

Medicine's little joke. Based on the old Egyptian method of halving a lemon and scraping out the inside, replacing the contents with honey and jamming it up inside you - pretending that maybe you put it in correctly in the first place and it's not going to slip - it is not exactly grounds for great foreplay like the packaging suggests. Some women have become one with their plastic citrus circles and can pop that spring into place in one try, but the rest of us are forced to excuse ourselves to the bathroom and grope around until we collapse into a sweaty exhausted heap on the bathroom floor. All this and no orgasm.

Sponges

Slightly less stressful than the diaphragm or cervical caps. Unfortunately, mostly because of human error, the success rate on them runs at about 70%, meaning that you still have a 30% chance of pregnancy. I wouldn't take those odds. Plus, there are few things that smell so foul as a freshly removed sponge. And they are very expensive for what they are.

IUDs

Surgically inserted, many of the new ones are supposed to be pretty decent. You run the risk of infection, however, in that there is a string that runs directly from the IUD to the vagina, potentially exposing your womb to any STDs you might encounter. This could very well render you infertile and is usually not inserted unless you suspect that you don't want any more munchkins.

Oestrogen and Progesterone pills, Norplant and hormone injections

Female hormonal contraception is truly a bureaucratic miracle. Most women experience some kind of negative side effect from the hormones: hair loss, weight gain, heavier periods, worsened cramping, spotting, headaches, blood clots, mood swings, depression and loss of libido. In all fairness, many women report relief from many of the same symptoms. However, the pill was put onto the market before all of the standard research had been completed. In fact, we will not know exactly what effect hormonal therapies have on women until the year 2005. This will be far too late for the first two generations of women who have been regularly put on long term hormone treatment starting with their first sexual partner and ending long after menopause. The reason for such irresponsibility is that some authorities (who are often compensated for prescribing the drugs) feel that increased hormones may help combat osteoporosis and aging. But they are not sure.

Another thing to keep in mind about hormone treatments is that because they alter your hormones and your cycle, they often blunt or even destroy your sex drive, rather defeating the entire purpose of being on the things.

In contrast, a few years ago in Boston a male pill was invented. It was discovered that some men who took one version of the hormones displayed slightly less facial hair than previous. The project was dropped.

Angry?

All this being said, hormone treatments are still the most effective means of contraception beyond sterilisation. The choice is yours.

Have a thought before using any means of contraception besides one or the other of the plastic bags. Have both yourself and your partner tested for every little nasty known to man. Decide how reliable you need your contraception to be. If 70% is good enough for you, aces, but be fully aware of the implications.

Lastly, it is O.K. to sleep with a man and then never to see him again. This doesn't give you permission to be cruel when he calls. It simply gives you permission to be busy. It is generally understood that it is the actions performed upon a man that determine the degree of pleasure experienced. For many women it is the emotion that they feel for the person that decides the intensity or mere existence of the orgasm. Men should understand that it is not that they are completely inept in bed or bad people; it's only that you didn't feel a thing.

Love

Love is great. It is the reason that mums change babies' nappies. It is why we keep animals, care for ailing parents, leave the lights on whilst making love. Love does not make the world go 'round, but it does make the ride more entertaining.

Lust is often mistaken for love. There is no sure-fire way to tell the difference between the two. Everybody has their own definition of love, and the way a person defines love is as variable as are people themselves.

Usually lust will fade. Love doesn't. It is easy to look back on a relationship and think that you were insane for ever loving that person. Don't worry, you probably didn't. Love will mutate. If the relationship ends or never really flies, these feelings may change into friendship love or enemy hate. If you are indifferent to the person, bravo, welcome to the lust septic tank.

Even true love will grow and change. The passionate love you feel at the beginning of a relationship will fade, and rightly so. We'd never get any work done if it didn't. You must accept that love runs in stages and evolves even, or perhaps mostly, within the healthiest of relationships.

There are some of us who get a case of the instant snuggle bunnies whenever a new person comes into our life. This isn't love, this is lust with a twist; falling in love with love. Those first feelings are nice and chemically addictive. And it's a fantastic idea, this love business. However, if you light up fast, you burn out even faster. If you are cautious you are far more likely to smoulder on for a while.

Don't jump into love, but don't push it away. For some people, love is a conscious decision, for others it's an awkward stumble down a never-ending flight of stairs. I know which I'd prefer.

Don't assume that there is only one man on this planet for you and that if you don't find him you will never be truly happy but will die in a big cold house with only your cat and your nieces and nephews for company, even though they are ungrateful brats who don't come by nearly often enough. The truth is that there are probably thousands of men with whom you could be happy. If you go through life thinking that if you try maybe just a little longer to find the exact right person for you, a guy who is precisely what you want him to be, you will be that pathetic old witch covered with cat hair. I'm not saying that you should settle; never *settle*, but be flexible. Stick to your guns on the things you know are of absolute importance and leave the rest to fate, whatever fate is.

How to Write a Love Letter

These are a little awkward. That's a lie. These are incredibly embarrassing for everybody involved and you will never ever live it down if anybody finds out during this lifetime. They're still going to be ragging on you in the hereafter and rightly so.

Having said that, if you must, keep it light. Say something silly about some quality that you genuinely admire. Tease and spar and be light-hearted. Write something really cheeky and stick it in his pocket, or slip it into his briefcase.

Never send a guy a letter asking him out or requesting him to do much of anything else. This is incredibly wimpy. Don't think he'll be able to overlook that.

Having said that, as you learned in the foreword, I chatted-up Michael Bywater via the Royal Mail with stellar results. Miracles like this do happen, but only to me.

Maybe think about just sending a succinct quote on the back of a postcard. Try something slightly obscure but somehow relevant. Something along the lines of 'Just whistle if you need me. You know how to whistle don't you? You just put your lips together and blow.' It doesn't matter if you don't get this exactly right (I didn't). If you feel awkward or shy about anything you write, you are doing the wrong thing. Stop.

Writing a Love Poem

Heavens preserve us, don't you dare. Everything I said before goes double for poetry. Again, if you must, plagiarise. It's easier in every way. Something sexual as opposed to romantic is also a good idea.

My favourite is 'i like my body when it is with your' by e.e. cummings (no, that is not a long stream of typos, cummings was something of a funny bunny). You read that poem and think about it enough and you won't even be needing yourself a man, Honey. Honest. It reads like an orgasm feels.

Also, think about using the lyrics from a favourite love song; preferably *Your song. Somebody* by Depeche Mode is good because it says just about everything about what anybody should want from their one and only. I particularly like the last line.

Alternatively, use a well known classic so they won't have to read the whole thing to get the gist.

As has been well documented, Elizabeth Barrett Browning was an embarrassing, lily-livered hypochondriac with an ego nearly as vast as her capacity for poor decision-making. But she had a swell heart and gave us one of the most famous first lines in poetry ever.

Sonnet XLIII, From the Portuguese

How do I love thee? Let me count the ways.
I love thee to the depth and breadth and height
My soul can reach, when feeling out of sight
For the ends of Being and ideal Grace.
I love thee to the level of every day's
Most quiet need, by sun and candlelight.
I love thee freely, as men strive for Right;
I love thee purely, as they turn from Praise.
I love thee with the passion put to use
In my old griefs, and with my childhood's faith.
With my lost saints, - I love thee with the breath,
Smiles, tears, of all my life! - and, if God choose,
I shall but love thee better after death.

Elizabeth Barrett Browning

It will give him plenty of room to reply with the
obvious: a poem by Robert Browning, Bitsy's ever so
much younger hunka-hunka burning love.

You

God be thanked, the meanest of his creatures
Boasts two soul-sides, one to face the world with,
One to show a woman when he loves her.

This I say of me, but think of you, love!
This to you - yourself, my moon of poets!
Ah, but that's the world's side, there's the wonder
Thus they see you, praise you, think they know you!

There, in turn I stand with them and praise you -
Out of my own self, I dare to phrase it.

But the best is when I glide from out them,
Cross a step or two of dubious twilight,
Come out on the other side, the novel
Silent silver lights and darks undreamed of
Where I hush and bless myself with silence.

Oh, their Raphael of the Madonnas,
Oh, their Dante of the dread Inferno,
Wrote one song - and in my brain I sing it,
Drew one angel - borne, see, on my bosom!

Robert Browning

If none of this appeals to you and you still want to send some poetry, Summersdale Publishers puts out a very nice book of love poems in both a hard and soft cover edition. *Classic Love Poems*, £10.99 hardback, £4.99 paperback.

Should you insist on writing your own, keep it light.

Spending Money

An important thing to remember when considering where to take a man on your first date: you invited him, so ethically, morally and probably you should pay. If you must you can go Dutch treat, but make that clear when asking him out, e.g. 'Do you want to go for ice cream, Dutch treat?' In any case, plan what your budget can comfortably afford.

If he insists on paying, let him. Don't get huffy, this has nothing to do with women's liberation. We are responsible for the continuation of the human race. At some point you will most likely, maybe not with him but with somebody, have to go through nine months of swollen ankles, not to mention the thirty odd years of the periodic P.M.T. that most women have to go through regardless of whether or not they choose to breed. No, it's not his fault, but I'm sure that if you asked God, She would fully endorse men's complete and total support of women in all aspects of life right from the early days on. So, if he wants to pay for dinner or open a door, let him. Consider yourself lucky for running into such an enlightened man.

Buy things for a man if you are wooing him. They don't have to be big things, flowers will suffice, or a bottle of wine. *They* have been doing it for ages. It will make him feel as highly valued as we do when it happens to us. And it's so much fun to see them blush.

How to Act in Front of His Parents

This is one of the few times when it is O.K. to alter completely and totally your appearance to make a good impression. Never ever show more skin than is absolutely necessary. Don't wear black. Take out your nose ring. Don't wear jeans or t-shirts or mini-skirts. If you own glasses, wear them. Be conservative. This is your family interview.

Always offer any help possible. Making dinner, setting the table, clearing the table, doing the dishes, washing the dog, anything. Don't be afraid of acting over eager. You can't fool parents, you should know better by now. They'll know that you're acting if you pretend to be nonchalant.

Most parents these days remember, or pretend to remember, the sixties. They will be nice, still recalling when they were cool and will probably want to remind you of it periodically.

Usually it is the mother with whom you will have the toughest time. There is a special bond between mothers and their sons and less progressive thinkers may feel that you are trying to steal their sons, even if their golden boys haven't lived at home for thirteen years and only come around at Christmas. There is not a lot that you can do with this sort of woman except try to be sympathetic and courteous.

Until very recently the most power women had was via their influence over men, being the 'power behind the throne'. This attitude extended to their sons. When you take their son in marriage you are dampening her influence and removing a portion of her power. You can see how an old dear might get a little huffy, even if her resentment is a bit misplaced and passé.

Check them out carefully as you are being vetted. When you marry a man (gasp!), you also marry his family. This may seem irrelevant whilst you are flitting through the marshmallow clouds of new love, but it will be important four years down the line when your in-laws move next door to be closer to the grandkids.

Watch how his family relates. This was the playpen in which he learned to form his own family. He may need a lot of work if his father's idea of good manners is to wait until after dinner to fart.

When Things Turn Sour . . .

Unfortunately the end result of many of even the most successful chat-ups is not the proverbial bowl of cherries but a sack of pips. You may soon realise that the instant rapport you felt with someone on the first evening was only your curry backing up on you and the chemistry was a barman who had a heavy hand with the vodka.

How To be the Nicest Possible Heartless-No-Taste-Wench-Who-Probably-Does-It-With-Donkeys around:

Sod's law has it that this man, whom you find to be a phenomenal bore with the fashion sense of your friendly neighbourhood pimp, thinks you are the bees knees and that the two of you would be best served by sharing the sheets for the rest of eternity. You must let him down gently.

If you have only seen each other a few times, it shouldn't be too much of a challenge simply to call and tell him that you got back together with your old boyfriend; you've eloped; you've been abducted by aliens who have altered your DNA patterns, thereby rendering him completely unattractive in your eyes; or that you are simply not interested - probably the kindest alternative.

After the first few dates things become far more complicated and painful. If you feel a relationship is winding down, don't try to fool yourself into thinking it isn't. This is most unkind and may send your now defunct love into severe confusion-based depression if he doesn't have some kind of previous indicator that this may not be your last stop on the Love Express.

In my youth of wine and roses I had a travesty of a break-up that unfortunately broke a very sweet heart. By my current scales we had something of a whirlwind romance, which climaxed in him putting an embarrassingly large diamond on my finger five months after he had placed a promise band on the said finger and nine months after our first meeting. We had been scheduled to be married eight months after the time that I broke up with him.

We had confessed passionate feelings for each other within a week of our first meeting and I suppose on some level I thought that I should stick to that. I wanted very much to be all grown up and he was nine years older and well established. Anyway, I realised one day when my entire family, my best friend and he were on holiday that I was in the middle of a lovely fantasy about my divorce and that I had been having nice thoughts about family lawyers in posh offices for nearly a year.

In a rare display of tact, I decided to wait until we were back from holiday to tell him of my revelation. Smart thing that he was, he realised that maybe I wasn't completely fine and forced the information from me.

So, following my own best advice, I asked for a trial separation and knowing me as he did, he said 'Cor blimey, not likely' and vomited all over the floor. In retaliation he has kept half of my furniture and most of my jewellry. I sneaked in and got back all of my kitchen appliances.

Admittedly, that was not a pleasant story, but it illustrates what a dire, chunky mess can be created by not being completely honest with yourself about your emotions all the way through a relationship. It is very easy to stick with a dead end relationship well past the comfortable stopping point due to your idealising of the situation in which you find yourself, and around which have already built some kind of a fantasy future. This isn't fair to either party.

If you feel that the relationship isn't nourishing but compromising you on some level, get out, fast. If you are feeling undervalued or unattractive because of your partner, have a good talk with him. If that doesn't result in positive changes in the behaviour of your partner, again get out, fast. An unhealthy relationship can screw you up emotionally for years. Don't be afraid to leave and never stay with someone through sheer habit. It is far better to be single than to be in a bad relationship.

Back to my own best advice: always offer a trial separation first. Who knows, you may discover during this time of little or no contact that a break was what you needed to appreciate the guy and that you are madly in love with him and can hardly believe that you were actually considering leaving this person for other pastures.

If you don't, at least he has had a warning; a transition period before he has to go into heavy-duty, alcoholic male denial.

There are men out there who may become obsessive, either because of the key scratch you put into the passenger side door of their ego or because they are romantics, or possibly both. It is easiest to get around if you were careful in making your initial selection and if you break it off nicely. If, after a month, he is still leaving poignant messages on your answering machine at three o'clock in the morning, change your number. If he is threatening you personally, get a restraining order.

Other than that, the only real advice to be given is act grown-up. And remember this too will pass and breaking off a relationship is nothing to feel guilty about, regardless of the reasons behind the split. At the end of the day, you have to do what is right for you. You are not going to be happy in a relationship that is destined for the bin and the longer you drag things out the more it's going to hurt.

After all of the drama is over, give yourself some time before searching for another man to give you regular rumpy pumpy. This is your mourning period. Even if he was a complete scoundrel and there is no question at all in your mind that you did the right thing, you still need to give yourself time truly to say goodbye to all of the dreams and expectations you had regarding this person. Don't close yourself off completely, but don't be afraid to tell someone that you are getting over a break-up and if you seem slightly out of focus, it's because you have just changed your film.

It's even OK to go into a fit of man hating at this point, just make sure that it is temporary.

How to Take it Like a (Wo)man When You Graduate to That-Mad-Bird-I-Broke-Up-With-Who-Gets-On-With-Mum-So-Well:

Never try to get them back into a relationship. This can't and won't work, not for the first year or so anyway, by which point I should hope that you are over it. It's humiliating and annoying and it will really irk all of your friends who already went through all of the *what do you think he meant when he said* at the beginning of the relationship and sure as sunshine don't want to listen to it again at the end when the results are so painfully predictable.

Don't cry on his shoulder about how much you're hurting. This is may be the most difficult part for a considerable number of people. Many couples become an entity unto themselves and find that when they break-up they haven't merely lost a bed buddy but a best friend and primary confidante. The breaker-upper will most likely humour this for a time, feeling that it is penance or out of respect for the dead relationship, but this is largely destructive as it reinforces an intimacy that can no longer exist. If you have no one else to talk to, hire a shrink.

Remember that the pain does go away and that there are other lovely things to do and see. Feel free to give yourself a little time when all of those lovely things will look a bit muddy and wilted. Be confident that a break-up is not something that should be taken personally. Oh, I know, how much more personal could it possibly get? But really, if they didn't like you they never would have come close enough to hurt you in the first place. Either they were the first to recognise that you simply were not compatible or there is something wrong with them.

You will feel better.

Astrology

A large number of people, mostly women, believe that their personalities and futures are determined by the alignment of planets and stars at birth. I am not saying whether it works or not, who am I to decide? So here are some basic compatibility and personality guides for the various signs of the western and Chinese horoscopes. This is very basic. If you want any more information, you can just sidle into your bookstore in dark glasses and a wig to get your *own* information.

Western

The first thing to understand about the western horoscope is that it is not based exclusively on sun signs, though these are the primary indicators. The other part that is supposed to contribute to making up the whole of your personality is the ascendant, based on your place, hour, year and day of birth. Combined they pinpoint the exact locations of the planets at the time of your birth and thus the nature of your person. If you want to have your entire birth chart done, it is not difficult. Hop in a car, drive to the worst part of town and ask where to find the woman with the most amusing fashion sense. If she doesn't do charts she'll probably at least be able to brew you up a good goat urine aphrodisiac.

For this purpose I will just go over the basic western sun signs and compatibility, leaving the complicated stuff to Madame Marge.

Aries

Aries is a very high energy, childlike sign; an aspect which often leads to selfish, but endearing behaviour. They have a short fuse, but are never angry for very long and will be surprised if you hold a grudge. They got over it, why don't you? They are highly competitive and like to think that they are breaking new ground and venturing through new frontiers in their chosen field. They revel in compliments, real or false and can be very cheeky.

Taurus

Taurus is a down to earth sign. Nothing is more important to the Taurian than settling down in their cozy little cottage with two point four children. They tend to be very possessive and often their partner will fall under this category. They can be very jealous and get their hearts broken often as they also fall into love easily in their typical Taurian attempts to get everything in their life settled. Taking everything in stride they tend to be easy going, provided that everything is meandering in a generally correct direction (think cow trail). It's difficult to push them too far, but once you have, hide (think stampede).

Gemini

Geminis are very highly strung, high energy people. They have to be as they insist on doing a dozen things at once. Geminis bore easily and are not keen on sticking to one task. They are born salespeople, but may never sell the same product the same way twice. They live their lives inside their heads, but are also very sociable. They may never say the thing that they happen to be thinking at the time. Variety is the spice of their lives, and this may also apply to their relationships, a fine thing if you don't mind being the flavour of the month.

Cancer

Cancerians are 'heart' people. Most things with them boil down to how they feel rather than what they think. Their homes and loved ones are the most important things in their lives, and they firmly believe that the way into a person's heart is through their stomachs, and will spend ages in the kitchen getting it just right. When they fall in love they fall hard and, in their tenacity, would rather cling to a bad relationship than admit defeat.

Leo

Leo is a born showman and likes always to be the centre of attention. She makes a much better leader than follower and hates to be cramped in by someone else's opinion. She loves to love and likes always to have something close at hand that needs her care and attention. This can take a nasty turn, however, as she can also become very patronising. She can get a little drunk on her own influence, but will usually control this fairly well.

Virgo

Virgos are very down-to-earth and intelligent. They do well in all kinds of service industries, particularly health care, as they have a fascination with the human body. They tend to be very tidy, unassuming and shy. They can also be very critical and sarcastic, but direct much of this negative energy upon themselves.

Libra

Librans are the defenders of fair play and hate selfishness in anyone. Those whom they love will be put upon a pedestal for as long as the Libran can push them up there. They will always believe the best of anyone they love and will stay in an unhappy relationship, as loneliness is one of their biggest fears. They need always to know that they have a good rapport with the people in their life, whether they be family, friends, colleagues, whatever. They love all beauty and adore luxury.

Scorpio

Scorpios are the Dick Tracys of astrology. Passionate people who like to come across as cold as ice. Sexy, suave, and secretive, they will channel this passion in any direction that seems attractive at the time as they are very scrummy. They can be controlling and should they ever be railroaded into a steady relationship, their partner had better be meek and learn to turn a blind eye to all that naughtiness.

Sagittarius

'Freedom' and 'optimism' are the two watch words when dealing with a Sagittarian. They really believe that if they have the right attitude they can make anything work. They love to travel and be out and about. They like to tell stories and hear themselves talk. They don't mean to lie, but their stories just seem to grow. Other than a few fish stories or even white lies, they are very honest, brutally so at times.

Capricorn

Capricorns tend to be serious. This doesn't mean that they don't have a sense of humour, only that it will be a bit dark, reflecting an inside that tends to be tied into knots much of the time. They will always look at the worst-case scenario, so if it happens they won't be too disappointed. They are actually very shy and have great difficulty expressing emotion due to fear of rejection. They can appear outwardly sociable, but it may take them ages to trust you enough to open up.

Aquarius

Aquarians are the wild children of the zodiac. They tend to be very intelligent and intellectual, good communicators. If there is a bizarre idea to be had, they are the ones who will have it. They love to be surrounded by people, but will not put up with stupidity or irresponsibility. They can be very stubborn and mulish when it suits them. They are completely unpredictable and charismatic.

Pisces

Pisceans tend to live their lives with their emotions very close to the surface. They are always at sixes and sevens and never seem really to have their heads screwed on straight. They tend to live in their own little worlds. Life is never as it seems to the Piscean, who will always change things around on the inside to suit what's on the outside. They are born romantics and will idealise their partners to the point of sainthood.

Compatibility Chart

Aries: Gemini, Leo, Sagittarius, Capricorn

Taurus: Virgo, Scorpio, Capricorn, Pisces

Gemini: Libra, Aquarius, Aries, Sagittarius

Cancer: Libra, Scorpio, Capricorn, Pisces

Leo: Aries, Sagittarius, Aquarius, Scorpio

Virgo: Taurus, Aquarius, Capricorn, Pisces

Libra: Aquarius, Sagittarius, Gemini, Cancer

Scorpio: Cancer, Taurus, Pisces, Leo

Sagittarius: Leo, Aries, Gemini, Libra

Capricorn: Virgo, Aries, Taurus, Cancer

Aquarius: Gemini, Virgo, Leo, Libra

Pisces: Cancer, Scorpio, Virgo, Taurus

Chinese Horoscopes

The complete reading of the Chinese horoscope is based on three different aspects. As with the western horoscope, the month in which you were born is significant, as is the ascendant. The main difference is that the year in which you were born is of primary relevance. Interestingly enough, the interpretations of the Chinese horoscope are largely similar to those of the western horoscope.

Monthly

For each month, roughly corresponding with the timing of the western horoscope, there is a different sign.

Aries   =   Dragon

Taurus   =   Snake

Gemini   =   Horse

Cancer   =   Goat

Leo   =   Monkey

Virgo   =   Rooster

Libra   =   Dog

Scorpio   =   Pig

Sagittarius	=	Rat
Capricorn	=	Ox
Aquarius	=	Tiger
Pisces	=	Rabbit

Ascendant

Always calculate your time of birth in terms of GMT time. Your interpretation, once again, can be read in the outline previously given of western horoscopes.

1am - 3am	Ox
3am - 5am	Tiger
5am - 7am	Rabbit
7am - 9am	Dragon
9am - 11am	Snake
11am- 1pm	Horse
1pm - 3pm	Goat
3pm - 5pm	Monkey
5pm - 7pm	Rooster

7pm - 9pm   Dog

9pm - 11pm   Pig

11pm- 1am   Rat

Year

In the Chinese horoscope this is supposed to be the primary contributor to your personality.

January 30, 1911-	February 17, 1912	Pig
February 18, 1912 -	February 5, 1913	Rat
February 6, 1913 -	January 25, 1914	Ox
January 26, 1914 -	February 13, 1915	Tiger
February 14, 1915 -	February 2, 1916	Rabbit
February 3, 1916 -	January 22, 1917	Dragon
January 23, 1917 -	February 10, 1918	Snake
February 11, 1918 -	January 31, 1919	Horse
February 1, 1919 -	February 18, 1920	Goat
February 19, 1920 -	February 7, 1921	Monkey
February 8, 1921 -	January 27, 1922	Rooster
January 28, 1922 -	February 15, 1923	Dog
February 16, 1923 -	February 4, 1924	Pig
February 5, 1924 -	January 23, 1925	Rat
January 24, 1925 -	February 11, 1926	Ox
February 12, 1926 -	February 1, 1927	Tiger
February 2, 1927 -	January 21, 1928	Rabbit
January 22, 1928 -	February 8, 1929	Dragon
February 9 1929 -	January 28, 1930	Snake
January 29, 1930 -	February 16, 1931	Horse
February 17, 1931 -	February 5, 1932	Goat
February 6, 1932 -	January 24, 1933	Monkey

January 25, 1933 -	February 13, 1934	Rooster
February 14, 1934 -	February 2, 1935	Dog
February 3, 1935 -	January 23, 1936	Pig
January 24, 1936 -	February 10, 1937	Rat
February 11, 1937 -	January 30, 1938	Ox
January 31, 1938 -	February 18, 1939	Tiger
February 19, 1939 -	February 7, 1940	Rabbit
February 8, 1940 -	January 26, 1941	Dragon
January 27, 1941 -	February 14, 1942	Snake
February 15, 1942 -	February 3, 1943	Horse
February 4, 1943 -	January 24, 1944	Goat
January 25, 1944 -	February 11, 1945	Monkey
February 12, 1945 -	February 1, 1946	Rooster
February 2, 1946 -	January 21, 1947	Dog
January 22, 1947 -	February 9, 1948	Pig
February 10, 1948 -	January 28, 1949	Rat
January 29, 1949 -	February 15, 1950	Ox
February 16, 1950 -	February 5, 1951	Tiger
February 6, 1951 -	January 25, 1952	Rabbit
January 26, 1952 -	February 13, 1953	Dragon
February 14, 1953 -	February 2, 1954	Snake
February 3, 1954 -	January 23, 1955	Horse
January 24, 1955 -	February 10, 1956	Goat
February 11, 1956 -	January 29, 1957	Monkey
January 30, 1957 -	February 17, 1958	Rooster
February 18, 1958 -	February 6, 1959	Dog
February 7, 1959 -	January 27, 1960	Pig
January 28, 1960 -	February 14, 1961	Rat
February 15, 1961 -	February 4, 1962	Ox
February 5, 1962 -	January 24, 1963	Tiger
January 25, 1963 -	February 12, 1964	Rabbit
February 13, 1964 -	January 31, 1965	Dragon
February 1, 1965 -	January 20, 1966	Snake

January 21, 1966 -	February 8, 1967	Horse
February 9, 1967 -	January 28, 1968	Goat
January 29, 1968 -	February 15, 1969	Monkey
February 16, 1969 -	February 5, 1970	Rooster
February 6, 1970 -	January 25, 1971	Dog
January 26, 1971 -	February 14, 1972	Pig
February 15, 1972 -	February 2, 1973	Rat
February 3, 1973 -	January 23, 1974	Ox
January 24, 1974 -	February 10, 1975	Tiger
February 11, 1975 -	January 30, 1976	Rabbit
January 31, 1976 -	February 17, 1977	Dragon
February 18, 1977 -	February 6, 1978	Snake
February 7, 1978 -	January 27, 1979	Horse
January 28, 1979 -	February 15, 1980	Goat
February 16, 1980 -	February 4, 1981	Monkey
February 5, 1981 -	January 24, 1982	Rooster
January 25, 1982 -	February 12, 1983	Dog
February 13, 1983 -	February 1, 1984	Pig
February 2, 1984 -	February 19, 1985	Rat
February 20, 1985 -	February 8, 1986	Ox
February 9, 1986 -	January 28, 1987	Tiger
January 29, 1987 -	February 16, 1988	Rabbit
February 17, 1988 -	February 5, 1989	Dragon
February 6, 1989 -	January 25, 1990	Snake
January 26, 1990 -	February 13, 1991	Horse
February 14, 1991 -	February 2, 1992	Goat
February 3, 1992 -	January 21, 1993	Monkey
January 22, 1993 -	February 9, 1994	Rooster
February 10, 1994 -	January 30, 1995	Dog
January 31, 1995 -	January 18, 1996	Pig
February 19, 1996 -	February 6, 1997	Rat
February 7, 1997 -	January 27, 1998	Ox
January 28, 1998 -	February 15, 1999	Tiger

Compatibility

This is based on a scale from one to eight, with eight being the most compatible. Handy to have all of these charts as you are bound to be compatible in at least one of the four aspects of astrology mentioned.

	Dra	Sna	Hor	Goa	Mon	Roo	Dog	Pig	Rat	Ox	Tig	Rab
Dragon	7											
Snake	7	7										
Horse	6	3	7									
Goat	6	4	7	7								
Monkey	8	3	4	4	7							
Rooster	7	8	5	4	4	3						
Dog	1	6	8	3	6	4	6					
Pig	6	1	6	8	6	4	6	6				
Rat	8	6	1	4	8	5	6	6	7			
Ox	6	8	5	1	4	8	3	5	7	6		
Tiger	6	3	8	4	1	5	8	7	4	3	6	
Rabbit	6	6	3	8	5	1	7	8	6	6	4	7

Scenarios

Pub/Bar

Your local can either be the best or worst place to chat someone up. It can be an excellent spot for networking and a flirt. You should probably consider your best option to be to start out in the pub or local wine bar, spot and chat-up some unsuspecting sweetheart and move onto a different venue.

The fortunate thing about bars and pubs is that people are very drunk and probably feeling companionable, and therefore won't be rude. There is a plethora of lines you can use that won't sound odd at any time.

Be sure to select your pub carefully. There will be your grandpa pubs, dart pubs, underage-Pepsi clubs and the like. The type you want will have a good cross section of people from the age of about eighteen to forty. A wine bar will usually have a healthy, diverse mix of people and will tend to not go in and out of favour in the way the pub scene does.

Introductions

Introductions covers many options, some of which people like to pretend don't exist.

You can run into a lot of weirdoes who put ads in the personals. You can also run into a lot of less than normal people in pubs, on the street, at work or on holiday.

People place ads in the personals for a variety of reasons. Their immediate circle of friends may have been leached of potential romantic conquests. The group may no longer have any second cousins to offer up. They may have an anti-social job that keeps them locked in a closet all day. Maybe they are new in town. They are not necessarily losers.

Having said that, if you decide to call someone who has splashed their compressed credentials all over *The Times*, be a little hesitant and cautious about your own approach. Don't give out your phone number or anything until you are very sure of the person, and maybe even until you have met them (during the day in a crowded place, of course).

By far the safest alternative when considering getting involved with any sort of introduction is to get in with some kind of an organisation that does group activities. I understand that Dinner Dates is one of the better of its kind. You are in a group, everybody is single, it is chaperoned and all of the members have been screened. What could be better?

Contrary to popular belief, the people who get involved in such things are not sad gits, although these organisations can be quite expensive to get involved in and often only the most affluent can afford them or need to use them, their main reasons being a lack of time and a want for something more fulfilling than their daily routine of paper shuffling.

Personal introductions via mutual friends are often very effective. The mutual friend can also act as a reliable go-between to feed you with inside information as to how much the other person hates you after the first date and whether you ought simply not to call him again or to emigrate.

Street

It can be very awkward approaching someone in the street, but everyone has to do it at least once. Don't show fear. Don't approach someone standing in the middle of a group of people and don't say anything stupid.

It is acceptable and not too embarrassing to approach someone in the street if you are both jogging. You are starting out with common ground and everybody can use a little company when you are doing something as mind-numbing as pounding the pavement.

If you are making good eye contact with someone approaching you and get a smile, take advantage of this opening and jump in there, pistols ready. Try never to let a case of the instant hot pants pass you by.

Nightclub

When going to a nightclub you have to have an attitude that permeates everything. You have to dress it, look it, smell it, taste it, feel it and drink it (mine's a double kamikaze on the rocks). To fit in truly and to be sexy in a nightclub situation you must feel that you are completely comfortable with the company you are keeping and with the place and its music. If you look and feel awkward, yes you will still attract men, but they are the type who are perhaps a little insecure, and like a woman to appear vulnerable. This is bad.

Chatting-up a man in a nightclub is something of an oxymoron. *Chatting* simply isn't possible. The music is too loud, the shadows are too dark and the drinks are too strong. The most you can do is tap them on the shoulder, grind your pelvis against theirs and ask if they would care to dance. It goes without saying that this is usually more than sufficient.

Use common sense and remember that there is a danger in taking home, or being taken home by a complete stranger. If you want to be sensible and stay alive for an extended period of time, get his phone number and call him after your hangover has run its course.

Parties

Don't be intimidated by parties. People are there because they want to be around their friends and meet new ones. That is the whole point. The trick to parties is to mingle. It isn't nearly so difficult as it sounds. Before approaching a group of people, carefully note their body language. If they are standing close together with their shoulders hunched forward, leave it alone, it's a private group. Instead, approach a group of three or more people where you can easily slip in and observe them and the conversation quietly before throwing in your own witticisms. If you are lucky you will locate a group with a member rude enough to drag you forcibly into a conversation.

In the beginning of the evening, walk into the room like you own it. Stand off to the side to allow other people to walk in and quietly observe the room, with a hint of an inviting smile on your face. Find a man who blows your skirt up (carefully checking his left hand for rings) and make it the goal of your evening to get into his small pants, or at least into the corresponding part of his brain. Be sure to talk to the whole group, but concentrate on him.

At a more intimate, thumping music sort of party, you might be best off trying to get them when they are alone, on their way to or from somewhere. You can offer them a drink without having to expend too much energy shouting over the music. Treat it like you would a nightclub, the difference being that you probably have a mutual friend and could get into a spot of trouble with them if you treat this person badly.

A party is also good in the sense that you can get this mutual friend to introduce you or, for the more subtle sort, to help manoeuvre you into the group they're with. Hope that you don't have one of those annoying drunk hosts who introduces people by saying clever things like, 'Oi, Joe, look it's Tina, you should ask her to take her tits out. I think she fancies you and I hear she bonks at least three men a weekend. I think you're in there, leave some for me, Mate.'

Office

I know that it is often recommended that office romances be avoided, but this is largely foolish advice. What better place to meet someone? You are there all day, you have at least one thing in common.

As previously mentioned in the chapter *Targeting*, don't get into this sort of relationship unless you are sure you can withstand the potentially painful aftermath.

I wouldn't recommend that you get into any sort of a casual relationship in this situation. You don't want to step on any toes or bruise any egos if you are going to be seeing this person with any degree of frequency. Make sure that you are both tuned into the same station and have the same hopes and expectations involving the relationship. Generally speaking it is best that you start out as friends and work your way up (or down).

Be very careful, but don't turn a man down just because he is at the workstation next to you. Try to keep the situation quiet around the office. If everybody knows it will be harder to get in and out of the relationship and could call up the attention of a disapproving, prudish superior who would prefer to keep exotic bodily fluids off of the photocopier.

Holidays

You have been saving for your trip to Crete for almost nine months. You bought bags and bags of close-to-co-ordinated separates. You endured session after session of electrolysis and lay out on your roof naked before departure in ten degree weather to minimise the grotesqueness of your jello thighs and sustained nipple burn. You don't want to waste this.

Almost any holiday romance is going to be short and sweet, that's the rules. Often you can leave off the sweet bit and replace it with the word 'sweaty', or 'anonymous'. It is a little quirk of circuitry that women often find they are able to behave on holiday the way men are purported to do daily. Maybe it is because you know very few of the locals in Crete and most of them don't understand a word that you are saying anyway.

Go for it, but don't automatically expect that there is any sort of rosy coloured letter writing future in it. The native boys are after a bit of slapping, tickling romance with the foreign girls primarily and probably because there is likely to be little to no commitment involved. Any real affection should be regarded strictly as a bonus.

Not to crash the romance of the whole thing, but EU and American passports are considered quite the commodity in many countries. I know that you are a 'mega sex' - not to mention bright, funny and wonderful - but if he seems awfully keen and pushy and instantly lovey and all that rot, don't exclude the possibility that he may be having trouble seeing you through all of the paperwork.

I find that most vacation spot romances die on me for no other reason than that the man's English is so bad he can't communicate a sense of humour. Some people don't have a problem with that, enjoying the challenge of having to really work at communicating 'would you like a drink' in sign language.

All that being said, holiday romances can be good fun, particularly if you don't mind having salt and sand rubbed into every pore of your body whilst watching that magenta sun go down over amber waters. If drinking sangria out of a hip flask and sleeping naked under the stars wrapped around the toned buttocks of a swarthy man after skinny dipping in scuba gear sounds as good to you as it does to me, go for it.

Clubs and Societies

If you are in a new town, looking to meet people of similar interests or are a sad pratt with an incredibly small to nonexistent circle of friends, then joining a society or club might be just the thing for you.

Tip No. 1: Don't join a sewing circle or anything with the word 'daughter' in it. It defeats the purpose and the only men you will ever meet will be the worthless sons who come with the elderly members to the annual Association rained-out picnic.

Tip No. 2: If you are interested in entomology, but aren't fond of the type of people commonly associated with the science (nerds, gourmet bug tasters, etc.), don't join this club. Clubs are about people, not activities. On the other hand, it would be a little odd to join a sailing club if you are afraid of the water.

Don't join a club exclusively for the purpose of man hunting. Think of it more as creating a base and networking towards other people. Don't concentrate strictly on the men in the group. Think also of the women (you could make some wonderful, popular friends) and of the activity in which you are supposedly interested. If you go to a meeting and find it to be completely dreadful, do not feel honour bound to continue going. On the same note, do not pay any fees until you have sampled a bit of what you may be getting into.

The Gym

It would seem to me that the gym is intimidating enough without trying to score, but go for it if you don't feel even just a little silly in lycra and a ponytail.

As a general rule, don't go for guys who are too toned. There are three potential reasons.

A: They might use steroids. This is bad. Don't tell anyone, but L.A. was buzzing a few years back with the rumour that a certain hunka-hunka Hollywood He-man had to have an implant of a highly personal nature because his pony was a little slow getting out of the corral after a few too many years of 'roids.

B: If they don't use steroids they are spending entirely too much time in the gym thinking about their bodies. This can't be healthy and Goddess knows it's boring.

C: If their bodies are really good from either means they are going to have egos bigger than their pectorals. Physical appearance will be vitally important to them, if not the most important thing. You don't want to have to compete with a man for the mirror every morning.

The gym's primary purpose for you should be you. If you start getting really spruced up for your workout, you're missing the point. It's best to consider it as the dressing room rather than the stage for chatting up.

If you're still making eyes at some goober, you could offer to spot him on the free weights, or ask him to spot you. You could place your step next to his at step class. You could catch him in the queue at the drinking fountain. It's up to you.

Library

People who go to libraries, read, and do research, are generally of an intelligent, serious breed. They probably don't think that you should talk in a library, or if you must, don't speak loudly.

Don't approach someone when they are sitting quietly, minding their own business, engrossed in whatever it is that they are reading. This could annoy them. Instead try talking to them when they are at the photocopier making a ton of copies. They will be bored to the point of suicide and won't have any objections at all to having a go at chatting with the sex queen they see before them.

Alternatively, if you are both waiting in line for the copier and you are making tons of copies while he only has a few, let him go ahead of you. Generosity is very becoming.

Libraries are confusing places, what with the Dewey Decimal system and all. Feel free to ask directions, or even their opinion if they seem the sort to have one.

There is always the possibility that the person you have your eye on, particularly in a student library, will be a regular and you can count on them often appearing at close to the same place at around that same time. In this case you can take the slow and sudden approach and sit near them a few times before finally starting a conversation. Be warned, if he spends a lot of time in the library studying, as opposed to researching, be probably lives in a very noisy house with a bunch of obnoxious roommates. You'd better make sure your own sheets are clean.

A bit of trivia for you: Bill Clinton and Hillary Rodham Clinton, President and First Lady of the USA at the time of writing, met in a library. Popular lore has it that when Bill and Hill were going to law school they were both spending an excess of time in the law library, as one does. Bill took a shine to Hillary and would arrange himself day after day so he could watch her. Finally Hillary, being my kind of girl, slammed her books down, marched to where he was sitting and demanded 'Can I help you?' They've been together ever since.

Supermarket

If you find a man in a supermarket he is either pregnant, lost, gay, responsible, or has been single for a suspiciously long time.

The pregnant man is there because his wife is in her ninth month and had a mad craving for pickled prawns and refused to leave the house because her ankles are swollen. She's fat and she hasn't a thing to wear. He knows that there isn't a chance in hell of her wanting the pickled prawns if he actually finds them, so he wanders around, grabbing various bits and pieces of other inedible food sold in small quantities just for this purpose, dreading going home. Sometimes he'll be standing in the middle of the store on a mobile phone looking incredibly patient and saying kind things about water retention.

The lost man is there. He doesn't know exactly why. His girlfriend gave him a list, but he left it in his jacket which he forgot in his friend Steve's hotel room, who lives in Canada and came over to check out the motorbike scene in the U.K.. He has a small shopping basket with him which is quickly filling up with *Cadbury's Mini Rolls*, Apple *Tango*, beef flavoured crisps, and beer. He knows that he is never going to grab the exact thing she asked for, but tries occasionally by dropping a pint of milk or a loaf of discounted bread into the basket. He looks sweet and vulnerable because he knows he's going to get it when he gets home.

The gay men are easy to spot. They are the ones reading the side panel on the box of muesli. Often they will be shopping with their partner and will be more than happy to help you unload your basket.

Responsible men are few and far between. They can often be mistaken for the gay men as they sometimes sneak a peak at the side labels of the cereal boxes. They buy actual ingredients for things that they could potentially cook in the future. The difference is that when they are helping you to empty your trolley they are doing it mostly so that they can have a more comfortable conversation with your chest.

The man who has been single for too long has a shopping style very similar to both the responsible man and the lost man. He usually has a trolley rather than a basket, but he never reads side panels and the only cereal he buys is frosted flakes. He usually doesn't buy actual ingredients, preferring to purchase items with the word 'Mother' clearly marked on the box. He buys large quantities of the same processed foods, but all in the small, expensive size.

If you see someone whom you fancy in a supermarket, don't leave it. Whilst most people do go to the supermarket at just about the same time of day on the same day of the week, you may have one of those rogue shoppers who goes only when the last wrinkly orange has been eaten. This could take a while, particularly with all of the great deals being offered at supermarkets right now, encouraging people to buy in bulk.

Don't ask him about cooking instructions.

A: he won't know,

B: he'll wonder why you can't read the package all by yourself.

Try instead to ask him if a particular food he is going to buy is generally edible or just a funny little addiction of his, as you have been thinking about buying it and didn't want to be the first guinea pig. It is best to do this in the wine section, because nobody really knows much about wine, particularly not if they are buying supermarket plonk. So you won't appear ignorant for asking and they assume that you must think they are quite something.

You can always try the old stand-by of bashing your trolley into his, but don't do it too hard. Any old chat-up line will do once you have his attention, beyond 'Mine's a gin and tonic.'

If it's a busy day, stand in the same line as his. He's bored too, and will most likely welcome any conversation. If all goes well you can always dump your stuff in the car and grab a coffee in the café. Not a good idea if your shopping included ice cream, however.

Public Transport

I always get stuck with vehicles filled with the least attractive, most toothless people in the population when I use public transport. If you have a different experience, please let me know so I can change my bus route.

This isn't saying that it is impossible to sit next to someone attractive on the plane to Rio, all I'm saying is that they're going to be either married, gay or female.

Plane

For the sake of argument, let's say it does happen. You are sitting in economy class on your way back from Malta where you got the most incredible tan. You were very good and stuck to salads and diet cokes and only gained three pounds. You are on a discount package, so you have a stop over in Rome between Malta and Gatwick. You've got the window seat and some old Greek lady who speaks no English, but keeps on showing you pictures of kids who are probably her grandchildren, is sitting in the aisle seat. It looks like a full flight besides the seat between you, and you are looking forward to taking full advantage of it and stretching out a bit. It's been a hectic two weeks.

Suddenly, from first class, you hear a huge fuss. You can't see anything because of the curtains, but someone is cursing very loudly in Italian. You studied Italian briefly whilst you were dating Mario at university, and are able to make out some of what the man saying. Apparently he booked a first class ticket, but his seat was mistakenly reserved for economy. It appears that first class is just as crowded as the cattle corral at the back.

The curtains are flung back and the stewardess hurries through the doorway followed by a tall dark man with incredibly broad shoulders who bears a striking resemblance to Clarke Gable, except for a pair of large cornflower blue eyes. You catch your breath as the stewardess directs Clarke to the seat upon which your cotton jumper is currently residing.

Mr. Gable angles in, his long legs cramped in the small seat. In perfect English he excuses that his leg is resting against yours. You blush prettily and tell him that no apology is necessary, but he might be well advised to speak with you until the granny is asleep, or be forced to look at pictures of drooling children. He smiles a wolfish grin and agrees.

You learn that his name is Antonio Ferrari of the original car making family and he is to be in London for several weeks to visit his mother, who is currently estranged from his father; that Italian temper. He will have a car and driver waiting at the airport, it would give him great pleasure to take you anywhere you might like to go . . .

But this never has and never will happen.

"And that's little Tommy..."

The same goes for Britrail and that Interail pass you were thinking of picking up next summer.

The night I wrote this my mother had a hen night for a few of her friends, a bunch of sexy ladies who have been married for twenty five years or more (the best source of information for anything you want to know about anything). They were able to come up with three stories between them about love at first sight on aeroplanes. The problem is this: I always expect to meet interesting people when I'm travelling. If I thought I was always going to be stuck next to grannies on the plane, I might occasionally get planted next to someone decent. It's a little like how if you look like death warmed over when you go to the grocery store there is bound to be a GQ convention in the dairy section. It's called *Sod's Law*.

Bus and Underground

Generally speaking, these are short trips. If you fancy someone, make your move quickly, even if it is only to slip your phone number into their hand whilst whispering in their ear with your minty fresh breath 'I find you very attractive, call me.'

If you are on a packed bus and are lucky enough to have a seat, you can reserve the one next to you when it is vacated and indicate that it is for them, or when you get up you can do something similar for their benefit, leaving the perfect opportunity for you to slip them your card.

The Lines

A

Are your legs tired? You've been running through my mind all day.

Aren't you a friend of . . . ?

(Feel a muscle, any muscle) All these curves, and me with no brakes.

Afternoon. How are you?

B

Before I buy you a drink, will you tell me your name?

Believe me, I've tried to come up with an original chat-up line, but it's really difficult. Now that I am already talking to you though, I might as well carry on.

C

Can I borrow your phone? My ex told me to call when I fell in love again.

Can I borrow ten pence? I want to call your mother and thank her.

Can I flirt with you?

Can I have directions? (To where?) To your heart.

Can I buy you a drink?

Can you tell me the time please?

Could you recommend a good chat-up line? (repeat whatever he says.)

D

Do you know where we are? Because I'm lost in your eyes.

Do you have the number for heaven? It looks like they've lost an angel.

Do you know what would look good on you? Me.

Don't drink the beer here. It's awful. Try . . . instead.

Do you fancy doing something next week?

Do you want to hear my best chat up line? (yes) That was it.

E

Every time I come here I see you. What is your name?

Every time I see you I promise myself I'll talk to you. Now I've done it.

Evening. How are you?

Er, hello. My name's . . .

F

Forgive me for being so forward, but may I introduce myself?

G

Got a light?

Going my way? Can I walk with you?

Going so soon? Stay a bit and let me buy you a drink.

H

How about I sit on your lap and we'll see what pops up?

(Put a little water on him) How about you and I go back to my place and get out of these wet clothes.

Hey, don't I know you?

How about I buy you a drink?

How about coming back to my place for a bit of heavy breathing?

Hi, shy guy. Someone once told me that the loneliest people on this earth are shy men and beautiful women. I thought I'd come over and put both of us out of our misery.

If I had created the alphabet I would have put 'U' and 'I' together.

I forgot my phone number, can I borrow yours?

I've never chatted anybody up before. Will you teach me?

I like every muscle in my body. Especially yours.

Is your daddy a thief? ('no') Then how did he steal the sparkle of the stars and put them in your eyes? (be ready with a snappy answer in case they say 'yes')

If I told you that you have a beautiful body, would you hold it against me?

Is it hot in here or is it just you?

I miss my teddy bear. Will you sleep with me?

I want you to melt in my mouth, not in my hand.

Isn't this boring? Let's go somewhere quiet where we can get to know each other.

It's funny, but I'm sure I know you from somewhere.

I don't normally do this sort of thing, but here is my card - I'd like to meet you sometime.

I've been trying for ages to work out what to say to you . . . that was it.

If you want me, all you have to do is say so.

I have been watching you dance. It occurred to me since neither of us can dance, maybe we could just sit down and have a drink.

J

(Look at his shirt label. When they say 'What are you doing':)
Just checking to see if you're my size

OR
Just checking to see if you were made in heaven

Just give me five minutes to chat you up, please.

Kiss me.

L

Let's go to my place and do all the things I'll tell everyone we did anyway.

Let's play Hillbillies. You be my brother and we'll inbreed.

Listen, I want to tell you something . . . (whisper in his ear, blowing lightly. Say that you aren't wearing any underwear or something equally racy.)

Let's get out of here,

Let's skip the awkward beginning and pretend that we have known each other for a while. So, how's your Mum?

M

My name's (_____). That's so you'll know what to scream.

My name's (_____), but you can call me lover.

Morning. How are you?

Maybe we could have a drink sometime?

May I have a drag on your fag?

Most guys are like public toilets; either vacant, engaged or full of crap. Which are you?

N

Nice hat. Can I have it?

Nice tie. It matches my duvet.

Nice shoes. Take me.

Nobody could tell me who you are, but I'm sure that I've met you before.

O

Oh dear, I told myself that I wouldn't fall in love tonight. You've just changed all that.

On a scale of one to ten, you have been voted a ten by everyone over there. How do you feel?

Obviously this isn't very original, but can I buy you a drink?

P

(Grab his bum) Pardon me, is this seat taken?

Please sit.

Personally I feel that we could have a much better time somewhere else.

Please talk to me so that creep over there will leave me alone.

Q

Quick, the lights are coming back on soon. Kiss me.

R

Ring me sometime. I have to go now, but here's my number.

Rather than stay here all evening, shall we go somewhere quieter?

S

So, how am I doing?

Some people can run a mile in four minutes, yet it took me an hour to cross the four yards separating us.

Shall we go somewhere quieter?

T

The word of the day is 'legs'. Let's go back to my place and spread the word.

That shirt would look great in a crumpled heap on my bedroom floor.

There is a party tonight. Want to come?

Tell me about yourself.

U

Under this sophisticated, charming shell lies a very shy person. Be gentle.

V

Virtually everybody here except for you is ugly.

W

What would you like for breakfast?

Would you be my love buffet, so I can lay you out on the table and take what I want?

Weren't you in Los Angeles in the summer of '93?

What would you do if you ever got chatted-up by a woman?

Will you let me buy you a drink? Or at least walk me to the bar. I left my glasses at home and am completely blind.

Will you marry me?

Xanthippe I'm not. I promise. (explain the Xanthippe was the shrewish wife of Socrates.)

You show me yours, I'll show you mine.

You must be a *Snickers* bar, because my eyes are truly satisfied.

You're lovely.

You're so hot you melt the elastic in my underwear.

Your daddy must have been a baker, 'cause you sure have a nice set of buns.

You probably think that I'm mad coming up to you like this, but I have this strange urge to buy you a drink.

'Yes' is my favourite word. What's yours?

You look happy. Have you just farted?

You look likely. Want to take a shower with me?

Z

Zabaglione is my favourite dessert. If you're nice you can come home with me for a taste.

Epilogue

So here we are. You have all of the tools, have you the courage to exploit them? It is OK if you don't, honest. These things are frightening and it is perfectly fine if you are intimidated by the whole idea of approaching a man. Give yourself some time. Practice on your dog or your younger brother's friends. Work up to the punch and go at your own pace.

It is not all about sex, as I am sure you have noticed. Sexiness is only one of the by-products of an overwhelmingly positive self-image. This is the first and most important thing in life whether you want to be a lone shepherdess or a famous courtesan. Work on your head and the rest will come around.

Follow the summery of tips listed below and you may just turn out dandy, Kid:

- Be confident that you are a valuable worthwhile person. It doesn't matter if you have never had a date or if you need two home phone lines. I will concede that, unlike the American constitution implies, not all people are created equal. This in no way implies however, that we cannot all achieve the things that will ultimately make us leg-humpingly happy, be it man, beast or very fast car.

- Don't be afraid to take risks. This is what it is all about. Think of how boring (or non-existent) life would be if Adam and Eve had done nothing but hang out in that garden of earthly celibacy for eternity.

- Be logical and consider the biological imperative before you get your heart broken or start snorting lust flavoured love. Using the tools in this book you can talk yourself out of almost any heartbreak or rejection, but only when you are ready. There is a lot to be said for a little suffering. That is how we learn.

- Don't think of being single as a negative state. It is simply an alternative, and a very comfortable one at that. During the time that you are single you can really get to know and be yourself. There is a whole lot to be said for the manless state of being.

- Appreciate that men are different and don't try too hard to figure them out. Everybody is different, sex is just one of the myriad of things that distinguishes one person from another. If you must analyse a man, don't tell him about it. As a rule he won't understand and will feel threatened if you know more about him than he does.

- Always know your ultimate purpose in talking to a man and don't settle for anything different. If you want to begin a committed relationship, don't settle for a night of sex and tequila. Oh fine, if you must, but it will smart something fierce.

- Don't take it personally if they turn you down. Obviously they aren't worth it and were not meant for you.

- Revel in what makes you different. It makes you you. Decide for yourself what is attractive and beautiful and make sure it's you. Don't let society make this decision for you.

- Call him. If he doesn't like it he wasn't worth it in the first place.

- Never pretend that you are anything or anyone other than the person you are. Fall in love with yourself and others will follow. Always be true to you.

- Learn to read the signs, whether they be *come here* or *go now*. Learn to send the same ones.

- Decide, with very broad parameters, what kind of a man you want. Stick with it. Never settle, but always be willing to compromise.

- Learn all that you can about sex and make some decisions about how you feel about it. You don't have to be a mega sex, but you don't need to be a prude either. Never do any more or less than you are comfortable with.

- Love is very subjective, and must be treated as such. Don't let anyone, including yourself, talk you into or out of it.

- Let all relationships die a natural death and give yourself the time you need to mourn. Don't force anything and never think that you are feeling anything wrong or bad. There is no such thing.

- Feel free to write your own rules.

Laugh hard and often. It is all so very *funny*.

A brief biography of Amy Mandeville

Amy is a graduate of a California State University, having majored in anthropology, the study of man, figuring that she might as well make her true purpose for going to university official. Since graduating at the tender age of nineteen, she has been travelling the world, tediously researching and compiling information for her masterpiece *How to Chat-up Men*.

After completing all of the necessary publicity surrounding the book, Miss Mandeville intends to settle into the glamorous world of freelance writing and blood worm farming with the biggest, stupidest man she can find.

Amy has completed and sold many freelance assignments, as well as a highly marketable thesis she is currently trying to sell the movie rights for entitled *The Instance of Coccidiodomycosis in the Native American Population of CA-CAL 629/30*. She is still waiting for the call.

Amy realised what an anthropological loophole there was in society when her Franco-Swedish blood would suddenly urge her to chat-up anything that walked past with three legs and her friends with less lusty constitutions would refuse to follow. It was then that it occurred to her that they simply didn't know how. This book is dedicated to all of those who didn't take the dare to walk on those watery knees.